T

NOTES

including
- *Life of Shakespeare*
- *Brief Synopsis of the Play*
- *List of Characters*
- *Summaries and Commentaries*
- *Character Analyses*
- *Questions for Review*
- *Selected Bibliography*

by
Waldo F. McNeir, Ph.D.
University of Oregon

INCORPORATED
LINCOLN, NEBRASKA   68501

Editor

Gary Carey, M.A.
University of Colorado

Consulting Editor

James L. Roberts, Ph.D.
Department of English
University of Nebraska

ISBN 0-8220-0052-0
© Copyright 1981
by
Cliffs Notes, Inc.
All Rights Reserved
Printed in U.S.A.

2000 Printing

Cliffs Notes, Inc.   Lincoln, Nebraska

CONTENTS

MERCHANT OF VENICE NOTES

LIFE OF SHAKESPEARE

Many books have assembled facts, reasonable suppositions, traditions, and speculations concerning the life and career of William Shakespeare. Taken as a whole, these materials give a rather comprehensive picture of England's foremost dramatic poet. Tradition and sober supposition are not necessarily false because they lack proved bases for their existence. It is important, however, that persons interested in Shakespeare should distinguish between *facts* and *beliefs* about his life.

From one point of view, modern scholars are fortunate to know as much as they do about a man of middle-class origin who left a small English country town and embarked on a professional career in sixteenth-century London. From another point of view, they know surprisingly little about the writer who has continued to influence the English language and its drama and poetry for more than three hundred years. Sparse and scattered as these facts of his life are, they are sufficient to prove that a man from Stratford by the name of William Shakespeare wrote the major portion of the thirty-seven plays which scholars ascribe to him. The concise review which follows will concern itself with some of these records.

No one knows the exact date of William Shakespeare's birth. His baptism occurred on Wednesday, April 26, 1564. His father was John Shakespeare, tanner, glover, dealer in grain, and town official of Stratford; his mother, Mary, was the daughter of Robert Arden, a prosperous gentleman-farmer. The Shakespeares lived on Henley Street.

Under a bond dated November 28, 1582, William Shakespeare and Anne Hathaway entered into a marriage contract. The baptism of their eldest child, Susanna, took place in Stratford in May, 1583. One year and nine months later their twins, Hamnet and Judith, were christened in the same church. The parents named them for the poet's friends Hamnet and Judith Sadler.

Early in 1596, William Shakespeare, in his father's name, applied to the College of Heralds for a coat of arms. Although positive proof is lacking, there is reason to believe that the Heralds granted this request, for in 1599 Shakespeare again made application for the right to quarter his coat of arms with that of his mother. Entitled to her father's coat of arms, Mary had lost this privilege when she married John Shakespeare before he held the official status of gentleman.

In May of 1597, Shakespeare purchased New Place, the outstanding residential property in Stratford at that time. Since John Shakespeare had suffered financial reverses prior to this date, William must have achieved success for himself.

Court records show that in 1601 or 1602, William Shakespeare began rooming in the household of Christopher Mountjoy in London. Subsequent disputes between Shakespeare's landlord, Mountjoy, and his son-in-law, Stephen Belott, over Stephen's wedding settlement led to a series of legal actions, and in 1612 the court scribe recorded Shakespeare's deposition of testimony relating to the case.

In July, 1605, William Shakespeare paid four hundred and forty pounds for the lease of a large portion of the tithes on certain real estate in and near Stratford. This was an arrangement whereby Shakespeare purchased half the annual tithes, or taxes, on certain agricultural products from sections of land in and near Stratford. In addition to receiving approximately ten percent income on his investment, he almost doubled his capital. This was possibly the most important and successful investment of his lifetime, and it paid a steady income for many years.

Shakespeare is next mentioned when John Combe, a resident of Stratford, died on July 12, 1614. To his friend, Combe bequeathed the sum of five pounds. These records and similar ones are important, not because of their economic significance but because they prove the existence of a William Shakespeare in Stratford and in London during this period.

On March 25, 1616, William Shakespeare revised his last will and testament. He died on April 23 of the same year. His body lies within the chancel and before the altar of the Stratford church. A rather wry inscription is carved upon his tombstone:

Good Friend, for Jesus' sake, forbear
To dig the dust enclosed here;
Blest be the man that spares these stones
And curst be he that moves my bones.

The last direct descendant of William Shakespeare was his grand-daughter, Elizabeth Hall, who died in 1670.

These are the most outstanding facts about Shakespeare the man, as apart from those about the dramatist and poet. Such pieces of information, scattered from 1564 through 1616, declare the existence of such a person, not as a writer or actor, but as a private citizen. It is illogical to think that anyone would or could have fabricated these details for the purpose of deceiving later generations.

In similar fashion, the evidence establishing William Shakespeare as the foremost playwright of his day is positive and persuasive. Robert Greene's *Groatsworth of Wit*, in which he attacked Shakespeare, a mere actor, for presuming to write plays in competition with Greene and his fellow playwrights, was entered in the *Stationers' Register* on September 20, 1592. In 1594 Shakespeare acted before Queen Elizabeth, and in 1594 and 1595 his name appeared as one of the shareholders of the Lord Chamberlain's Company. Francis Meres in his *Palladis Tamia* (1598) called Shakespeare "mellifluous and hony-tongued" and compared his comedies and tragedies with those of Plautus and Seneca in excellence.

Shakespeare's continued association with Burbage's company is equally definite. His name appears as one of the owners of the Globe in 1599. On May 19, 1603, he and his fellow actors received a patent from James I designating them as the King's Men and making them Grooms of the Chamber. Late in 1608 or early in 1609, Shakespeare and his colleagues purchased the Blackfriars Theatre and began using it as their winter location when weather made production at the Globe inconvenient.

Other specific allusions to Shakespeare, to his acting and his writing, occur in numerous places. Put together, they form irrefutable testimony that William Shakespeare of Stratford and London was the leader among Elizabethan playwrights.

One of the most impressive of all proofs of Shakespeare's authorship of his plays is the First Folio of 1623, with the dedicatory verse which appeared in it. John Heminge and Henry Condell, members of Shakespeare's own company, stated that they collected and issued the plays as a memorial to their fellow actor. Many contemporary poets contributed eulogies to Shakespeare; one of the best known of these poems is by Ben Jonson, a fellow actor and, later, a friendly rival. Jonson also criticized Shakespeare's dramatic work in *Timber: or, Discoveries* (1641).

Certainly there are many things about Shakespeare's genius and career which the most diligent scholars do not know and cannot explain, but the facts which do exist are sufficient to establish Shakespeare's identity as a man and his authorship of the thirty-seven plays which reputable critics acknowledge to be his.

BRIEF SYNOPSIS OF THE PLAY

Antonio, a leading merchant of Venice, is a wealthy, respected, and popular man. Among his many friends is a young man named Bassanio, who owes Antonio a good deal of money. Bassanio would like to repay his friend, but so far he has been unable to do so. However, he now feels that he may have found a way – but he will again need a loan from Antonio. In Belmont, Bassanio tells Antonio, there lives a beautiful and young and wealthy heiress. Bassanio feels sure that he can win her hand in marriage, but he cannot go courting "hands-hanging." If he is to make a good impression, he has to appear at least as well off as her other wealthy suitors. Antonio tells his young friend that he would gladly lend him whatever amount of money he needs, but at the present time he himself is short of cash. All of his money is tied up in his merchant ships, which are still at sea. However, Antonio will not disappoint Bassanio. He knows of a moneylender who will probably lend him the necessary amount, and Bassanio can use Antonio's good name as security for the loan.

At Belmont, Portia speaks to Nerissa, her confidante, telling her how tired she is of the constant stream of suitors, and how she wishes to be free of the perverse obligation of her father's will: Portia cannot choose her own husband; she can marry only the man who chooses the correct one of three caskets—one gold, one silver, and one lead; one contains her portrait and that one is the lucky casket. So far, none of her suitors has decided to risk choosing one of the caskets, which is all for the good, because Portia has no liking for any of them. However, when Nerissa mentions the name of Bassanio, a possible suitor, Portia's mood brightens. He was once a visitor at Belmont, and Portia was impressed with him.

Meanwhile in Venice, Shylock, a rich Jewish moneylender who harbors a secret hatred for Antonio, has agreed to lend Bassanio three thousand ducats for three months, on Antonio's bond. Foregoing his usual high interest rate, Shylock demands instead that if the day for payment falls due and the money is not returned, he may cut off one pound of flesh from Antonio's body. Antonio agrees because all of his ships are due back in Venice a full month before the bond falls due.

A romantic subplot develops when Lorenzo, a close friend of Antonio and Bassanio, falls in love with Shylock's daughter, Jessica. He manages to elope with her by disguising her as a boy, and she manages to take with her a goodly amount of her father's ducats. Of course, this infuriates Shylock, and he vows revenge. Shortly thereafter, Bassanio and Gratiano leave for Belmont, where the "fair Portia" has just sent away the Prince of Morocco and the Prince of Arragon, two more disappointed, unsuccessful suitors. When Bassanio asks to choose one of the caskets, Portia falls immediately in love with him, and she begs him to wait a few days before choosing one of the caskets. He has fallen in love with Portia and insists on taking his chances. He rejects the gold one, then the silver one; he chooses, finally, the lead casket, and on opening it, he finds a portrait of Portia. Both he and Portia are overjoyed, and they make plans to be married at once, along with Nerissa and Gratiano, who have also fallen in love. Happiness reigns in Belmont until Bassanio is brought a letter from Antonio bidding him farewell since his ships have been lost at sea and since it is impossible that he will live after Shylock collects his pound of flesh. Horrified, Bassanio leaves instantly for Venice with money which Portia gives him to pay the bond.

In Venice, Shylock is no longer interested in the mere payment of the money due him. He wants revenge. A Christian stole his daughter (and she took his money), and nothing will satisfy Shylock except the legal fulfillment of the bond. In the court of justice, presided over by the Duke of Venice, Shylock faces his enemy, Antonio. Antonio is surrounded by his friends and is quietly resigned to death. On all sides, Shylock is surrounded by enemies. Bassanio pleads with Shylock to accept double the money due him, but Shylock refuses.

At this point, Portia, disguised as a lawyer, and Nerissa, dressed as her law clerk, enter the court and tell the Duke that they have been sent from Padua by a learned attorney, Doctor Bellario, to plead the defendant's case. Portia entreats Shylock to be merciful, but he will not listen. She offers the moneylender *triple* the amount owed him, but again Shylock will have none of it. She then solemnly informs the court that Shylock is entirely within his lawful rights. She then informs Shylock that he must be very careful. He must cut off *exactly* one pound of flesh, and he must not spill one *drop* of Antonio's blood. If he fails, all of Shylock's lands and goods will be confiscated. Shylock hastily decides that he will accept the triple payment of the bond, but Portia says *no*; Shylock then offers to take only the original three thousand ducats, but again Portia refuses, reminding him that it was he himself who demanded the strict interpretation of the law. Furthermore, she says, the law has another hold on him. Since he is an alien in Venice and since he tried to "seek the life" of a Venetian citizen, all his wealth can be divided between the citizen whom he attempted to destroy and the public treasury; in addition, Shylock's own life is in peril because of what he attempted to do.

The Duke decides to spare Shylock's life, but he does give half of Shylock's money to Antonio, and he gives the rest of it to the state. Antonio says that he will not accept the money if Shylock will agree to become a Christian and if, in his will, he will agree to leave his money to his daughter, Jessica, and her new husband, Lorenzo. Shylock, broken and defeated, agrees to all these conditions and leaves the court. Overjoyed, Antonio and his friends offer to pay the young lawyer whatever they can, but, oddly enough, the lawyer wishes only a certain ring which Bassanio is wearing. Bassanio is embarrassed because his wife gave this ring to him and asked him to wear it always. But the lawyer insists and, finally, Bassanio reluctantly gives away Portia's ring. Nerissa likewise cleverly manages to get from Gratiano a ring she gave him. The two ladies then hasten back to Belmont to tease their husbands about the rings.

When Bassanio and Gratiano, along with Antonio, return to Belmont, their wives inquire about the missing rings. Portia and Nerissa insist that the men no doubt gave the rings away to two other women. The husbands swear that it is not true, and it is not until Portia and Nerissa have put their husbands through some long, comically agonizing moments of discomfort that they confess that they themselves were the "learned doctor" and the "clerk" to whom the rings were given. Thus all ends happily, as Portia gives Antonio a letter informing him that three of his ships have arrived safely in port.

LIST OF CHARACTERS

Antonio

A wealthy Venetian merchant who occasionally lends money, but never charges interest. Since his main source of income is from his merchant ships, he is the "merchant" of the play's title.

Bassanio

He is a typical Elizabethan lover and nobleman who is careless with his money; hence, he has to borrow from Antonio so that he can woo Portia in style.

Portia

As one of Shakespeare's most intelligent and witty heroines, she is famous for her beauty and for her wealth, and she is deeply anguished that she must marry only the man who chooses the single casket of three which contains her portrait.

Shylock

Shylock is an intelligent businessman who believes that, since he is a moneylender, charging interest is his right; to him, it makes good business sense.

The Duke of Venice

He presides as judge over the court proceedings in Shylock's claim on Antonio.

The Prince of Morocco

One of Portia's suitors; he loses the opportunity to marry her when he chooses the golden casket.

The Prince of Arragon

He chooses the silver casket; he is another disappointed suitor for Portia's hand in marriage.

Gratiano

He is the light-hearted, talkative friend of Bassanio, who accompanies him to Belmont; there, he falls in love with Portia's confidante, Nerissa.

Lorenzo

He is a friend of Antonio and Bassanio; he woos and wins the love of Shylock's daughter, Jessica.

Jessica

She is the young daughter of Shylock; she falls in love with Lorenzo and, disguised as a boy, she elopes with him.

Nerissa

Portia's merry and sympathetic lady-in-waiting.

Salarino

He is a friend who believes that Antonio is sad because he is worried about his ships at sea.

Salanio

He is another friend of Antonio; he thinks Antonio's melancholy may be caused because Antonio is in love.

Salerio

A messenger from Venice.

Launcelot Gobbo

He is a "clown," a jester, the young servant of Shylock; he is about to run away because he thinks Shylock is the devil; eventually, he leaves Shylock's service and becomes Bassanio's jester.

Old Gobbo

The father of Launcelot, he has come to Venice to seek news of his son.

Tubal

He is a friend of Shylock's; he tells him that one of Antonio's ships has been wrecked.

Leonardo

Bassanio's servant.

Balthasar

The servant whom Portia sends to her cousin, Dr. Bellario.

Dr. Bellario

A lawyer of Padua.

Stephano

One of Portia's servants.

14

SUMMARIES AND COMMENTARIES

ACT I – SCENE 1

Summary

Walking along a street in Venice, Antonio (the "merchant" of the title) confesses to his friends Salarino and Salanio that lately he has felt unaccountably sad. They have noticed it, and they suggest that Antonio is probably worried about the safety of his merchant ships, which are exposed to storms at sea and attacks by pirates. Antonio denies this and also denies that he is in love, a possibility that both of his friends think might explain Antonio's pensiveness. Salarino concludes that Antonio's moodiness must be due simply to the fact that Antonio is of a naturally melancholy disposition. At this point, their friends Bassanio, Lorenzo, and Gratiano join them, and after an exchange of courtesies, Salarino and Salanio excuse themselves. Gratiano takes a long look at his old friend Antonio and playfully chides him for being so solemn and so unduly silent. Gratiano says that he himself never has "moods"; in contrast to Antonio, Gratiano is determined to always "play the fool." Lorenzo intimates that sometimes Gratiano is too much the fool – that is, he is too loquacious. He and Gratiano depart, promising to meet the others at dinner.

Left alone with Antonio, Bassanio assures him that he should not worry about Gratiano's critical remarks. Antonio then changes the subject abruptly; he asks Bassanio for more information, as promised, about the certain lady to whom Bassanio has sworn "a secret pilgrimage." Bassanio does not answer Antonio directly; he begins a new subject, and he rambles on about his "plots and purposes" and about the fact that he has become so prodigal about his debts that he feels "gag'd."

Antonio tells his friend to get to the point; he promises to help him if he can. Bassanio then reveals his love for the beautiful and virtuous Portia, an extremely wealthy young lady who lives in Belmont. He says that her beauty and her fortune are so well known, in fact, that she is being courted by "renowned suitors" from all parts of the world. Bassanio, however, is confident that if he could spend as much money as is necessary, *he* could be successful in his courtship. Antonio understands Bassanio's predicament, but Antonio has a problem of his own. Since all the capital which Antonio possesses has been invested in his ships, his cash flow is insufficient for any major investments at this time. As a solution, however, Antonio authorizes Bassanio to try to raise a loan using Antonio's good name as collateral for credit. Together, they will do their utmost and help Bassanio to go to Belmont in proper style.

Commentary

The first task confronting any playwright in his opening scene is his "exposition" of that play – that is, he must identify the characters and explain their situation to the audience. Shakespeare accomplishes this task of informative exposition very subtly in the opening fifty-six lines of dialogue between Antonio, Salarino, and Salanio. We learn that Antonio is a wealthy merchant; that he is worried for some obscure reason which makes him melancholy; that he is a member of a group of friends who arrive later – Bassanio, Lorenzo, and Gratiano – who represent the lively, convivial life of Venice. And perhaps most important for the purposes of the plot, we are told that Antonio has many shipping "ventures" – mercantile risks – and although he is not worried about them now, the idea is subtly suggested to us that his business ventures on the high seas *may* miscarry. We should recall this matter when Antonio finally decides to indebt himself to Shylock on Bassanio's behalf.

In this opening scene, Shakespeare begins to sketch in some of the characters and some of the atmosphere of the play. Antonio, for example, is presented as being "sad," afflicted with a melancholy which he himself does not appear to understand. Critics have puzzled over this: is Antonio to be viewed as a normally melancholy character? Is his sadness caused by his knowledge that he may shortly lose the companionship of his old friend Bassanio, who has told him of embarking on a "secret pilgrimage" to woo a beautiful and wealthy woman in Belmont? Or is his mood to be put down simply to an ominous foreboding which he has of some approaching disaster? For all dramatic purposes, in this scene Antonio's gravity serves, foremost, as a contrast to the lightheartedness of his friends.

Despite its dark and threatening moments, one should always remember that *The Merchant of Venice* is a romantic comedy and, like most of Shakespeare's romantic comedies, it has a group of dashing, if not very profound, young men. For example, Salanio and Salarino are not terribly important. Their lines are interchangeable, and they are not really distinguishable from one another. They represent an element of youthful whimsy. Salarino begins, typically, with a flight of fancy in which Antonio's ships are described as being like "rich burghers on the flood" and like birds, flying "with their woven wings." He continues into a delightfully fantastic series of imaginings; on the stage, of course, all this would be accompanied with exaggerated gestures, intended to bring Antonio out of his depression.

Thus, through the presentation on the stage of the sober, withdrawn Antonio, surrounded by the frolicsome language and whimsy of the two young gallants, Shakespeare suggests in compressed form two of the elements of the play—the real dangers that the merchant of Venice will face and the world of youth and laughter which will be the background to the love stories of Bassanio and Portia, Lorenzo and Jessica, and Gratiano and Nerissa.

This same note of gentle raillery is carried on when we see the entrance of three more young courtiers—Bassanio, Gratiano, and Lorenzo. Again, Antonio's mood is remarked on. Here again, Shakespeare is using Antonio as a foil for the spirited byplay of the others. Gratiano, especially, is ebullient and talkative, yet he is quite aware of his effervescence; he announces that he will "play the fool"; Gratiano talks, Bassanio tells Antonio, "of nothing, more than any man in all Venice," and his willing accomplice is Lorenzo; significantly, both of these characters are more distinctly drawn than Salanio or Salarino, and they will play more major roles in the development of the romantic plot and subplot of the play—Gratiano with Nerissa, and Lorenzo with Jessica.

One of the major purposes of this opening scene is to introduce Bassanio and his courtship of Portia, which will constitute the major romantic plot and also set the "bond story" in motion. Antonio's question concerning Bassanio's courtship of Portia is turned aside by Bassanio; he goes directly to the question of money, in order that the basis for the bond story can be laid. Some critics have seen in Bassanio's speeches some evidence of a character who is extremely careless of his money and very casual about his obligations; he seems, furthermore, to have no scruples about making more requisitions of a friend who has already done much for him. Yet clearly Shakespeare does not intend us to level any harsh moral judgments at Bassanio. According to the Venetian (and Elizabethan) view, Bassanio is behaving as any young man of his station might be expected to behave; he is young, he is in love, and he is broke. The matter is that simple. Antonio's immediate reassurance to his old friend reminds us of the strong bond of friendship between the two men. Interestingly, neither of them seems to be unduly concerned about money at this point; one is a wealthy merchant and the other, a carefree young lover.

This is a quality which we shall notice throughout the play in connection with both Bassanio and Portia; both of them recognize the necessity of money, but neither of them considers money to be of any value in itself. In their world of romantic love and civilized cultivation, they feel that they don't need to be unduly concerned with money. Shakespeare is setting up this point of view to contrast later with Shylock's diametrical point of view. For Shylock the moneylender, money constitutes his only defense against his oppressors.

Considering again Bassanio's problem with money and Antonio's reaction to it, note that Bassanio is straightforward in this scene with Antonio. His request is made "in pure innocence," and we take it at its face value. Those critics who decry Bassanio read more into his frank confession of poverty and his attempt to borrow money than is really there. We must recall that when Shakespeare wants to make us aware of some defect in one of his characters, he is always able to do so. The absolute and unconditional friendship between Antonio and Bassanio is one of the assumptions of the play, and we must never question it.

ACT I – SCENE 2

Summary

At Belmont, Portia discusses the terms of her father's will with her confidante, Nerissa. According to the will of her late father,

Portia cannot marry a man of her own choosing. Instead, she must make herself available to all suitors and accept the one who chooses "rightly" from among "three chests of gold, silver and lead." Nerissa tries to comfort Portia and tells her that surely her father knew what he was doing; whoever the man might be who finally chooses "rightly," surely he will be "one who shall rightly love." Portia is not so certain. None of her current suitors is the kind of man whom she would choose for herself *if* she could choose. She cannot, however, for she gave her word that she would be obedient to her father's last wishes.

Nerissa asks her to reconsider the gentlemen who have courted her, and she names the suitors who have come to Belmont – a Neapolitan prince; the County Palatine; a French lord, Monsieur Le Bon; a young English baron, Falconbridge; a Scottish lord; and a young German, the Duke of Saxony's nephew. Portia caustically comments on their individual faults, finding each one of them undesirable as a husband. Fortunately, all of them have decided to return home, unwilling to risk the penalty for choosing the wrong casket – which is, remaining a bachelor for the rest of their lives.

Nerissa then reminds her mistress of a gentleman who came to Belmont while Portia's father was living – his name was Bassanio, a Venetian, a scholar and a soldier. Portia recalls him and praises him highly: "He, of all the men that ever my foolish eyes looked upon, was the best deserving of a fair lady." A servant interrupts the conversation and announces that a new suitor, the Prince of Morocco, will arrive that evening.

Commentary

First off, the opening of this scene is deliberately reminiscent of the opening of Scene 1. Like Antonio, Portia announces her sadness, but unlike Antonio's, Portia's sadness is clearly due to the conditions imposed on her by her dead father's will: in the matter of her marriage, she must abide by the test of the choice of the three caskets; she can "neither choose who I would nor refuse who dislike [as a husband]."

We had been led to expect that Portia would be a woman who was very beautiful and very rich, but what we have now before us is a woman who is not only fair but quite impressive for her *wit*, for her agility of mind and for her sharp, satiric intelligence. It is, in fact, Portia's satiric flair that provides this comedy with most of its sparkle; here, it is displayed brilliantly when Nerissa urges Portia to reconsider her various suitors thus far, and Portia offers her wry and droll comments on each one.

It is at this point that Shakespeare is giving his audience the conventional Elizabethan satiric view of the other European nations. Portia's dismissal of each of her suitors corresponds to her age's caricatures of the typical Italian, Frenchman, German, and so on. The Neapolitan prince "does nothing but talk of his horse," a characteristic of only the *southern* Italian; the "County Palatine" (from the Rhineland) is a pure, unadulterated dullard; he is unable to laugh at anything; "Monsieur le Bon" is "every man in no man" — that is to say, he has many superficial and changeable characters but no single, substantial one. (To marry him, as Portia says, would be "to marry twenty husbands.") The English suitor, on the other hand, affects European fashions in clothing but gets all of the various national fads — in clothes, music, literature, etc. — completely confused, and refuses to speak any language except his own. And then there is the Scot — defined by his anger at the English; and finally, there is the German who does nothing but drink. Portia sensibly refuses to be married to a "sponge."

Basically, we can say that this scene has three major purposes. First, it outlines the device of the caskets for us, which will provide the dramatic basis for the scenes in which the various suitors "hazard" their choice of the proper casket for Portia's hand in marriage. Second, it introduces us to Portia — not simply as the "fair" object of Bassanio's love, but as a woman of powerful character and wit, perceptive about the people around her and quite able to hold her own in verbal combat with anyone in the play. This is a very important quality, given Portia's subsequent importance in the development of the plot. Her brilliance much later in the play, as a result, will not come as a surprise to the audience, especially when she superbly outwits the crafty Shylock. Finally, there is a minor but significant touch toward the end of the scene, when Nerissa asks Portia whether or not she remembers a certain "Venetian, a scholar and a soldier" who had earlier visited Belmont. First, we hear Portia's immediate recall of Bassanio, indicating her vivid memory of him and implying an interest in him. This scene reminds us that, despite the obstructions to come, this *is* a comedy, and that because of Bassanio's attempt to win Portia and her affection for him, both of them will be finally rewarded.

ACT I – SCENE 3

Summary

Bassanio seeks out Shylock, a Jewish moneylender, for a loan of three thousand ducats on the strength of Antonio's credit. Shylock is hesitant about lending Bassanio the money. He knows for a fact that Antonio is a rich man, but he also knows that all of Antonio's money is invested in his merchant fleet. At the present time, Antonio's ships are bound for distant places, and therefore vulnerable to many perils at sea. Yet he says finally, "I think I may take his bond." He refuses Bassanio's invitation to dinner, however; he will do business with Christians, but it is against his principles to eat with them.

When Antonio suddenly appears, Shylock (in an aside) expresses contempt for him, saying that he hates Antonio because he is a Christian, but *more important*, he hates Antonio because Antonio lends money to people without charging interest; moreover, Antonio *publicly* condemns Shylock for charging excessive interest in his moneylending business. Finally, though, Shylock agrees to lend Bassanio the three thousand ducats. Antonio then says that he – as a rule – never lends nor borrows money by taking or giving interest. Yet because of his friend Bassanio's pressing need, Antonio is willing to break this rule. The term of the loan will be for three months, and Antonio will give his bond as security.

While Bassanio and Antonio are waiting to learn the rate of interest which Shylock will charge for the loan, Shylock digresses. He tells them about the biblical story of how Jacob increased his herd of sheep. He calculates the interest which he will charge and announces: "Three months from twelve; then, let me see; the rate. . . ." Shylock then accuses Antonio of having repeatedly *spit* upon him and called him a *dog*. And now Antonio and Bassanio come asking him for money. Yet they pride themselves that Antonio is a virtuous man because he lends money to friends, with no interest involved. Is this loan, Shylock inquires, a loan to be arranged among "friends"? On the contrary; this is *not* to be regarded as a loan between friends, Antonio asserts. In fact, Antonio says, Shylock may regard it as a loan to an enemy if he wishes. Then, surprisingly, Shylock says that he *wants* Antonio's friendship, and to prove it, he will advance the loan without charging a penny of interest. But in order to make this transaction "a merry sport," Shylock wants a penalty clause providing that if Antonio fails to repay the loan within the specified time, Shylock will have the right to cut a "pound of flesh" from any part of Antonio's body. Bassanio objects to his friend's placing himself in such danger for his sake, but Antonio assures him that long before the loan is due that some of his ships will return from abroad and that he will be able to repay the loan three times over. Shylock insists, at this point, that the penalty is merely a jest. He could gain nothing by exacting the forfeit of a pound of human flesh, which is not even as valuable as mutton or beef. The contract is agreed to, and despite Bassanio's misgivings, Antonio consents to Shylock's terms.

Commentary

This scene has two important functions. First, it completes the exposition of the two major plot lines of the play: Antonio agrees to Shylock's bond – three thousand ducats for a pound of flesh; and second, and more important dramatically, this scene introduces Shylock himself. In this scene, Shakespeare makes it clear at once why Shylock is the most powerful dramatic figure in the play and why so many great actors have regarded this part as one of the most rewarding roles in all Shakespearean dramas.

Shylock enters first; Bassanio is following him, trying to get an answer to his request for a loan. Shylock's repetitions (Well . . . three months . . . well") evade a direct answer to Bassanio's pleas, driving Bassanio to his desperately impatient triple questioning in lines 7 and 8; the effect here is similar to an impatient, pleading child badgering an adult. Throughout the whole scene, both Bassanio and Antonio often seem naive in contrast to Shylock. Shylock has something they want – money – and both Antonio and Bassanio think that they should get the loan of the money, but neither one of them really understands Shylock's nature.

In reply to Bassanio's demand for a direct answer, Shylock still avoids answering straightforwardly. Shylock knows what he is doing, and he uses the time to elaborate on his meaning of "good" when applied to Antonio. Only after sufficient "haggling" does he finally reveal his intentions: "I think I may take his bond." At Antonio's entrance, Shylock is given a lengthy aside in which he addresses himself directly to the audience. Shakespeare often uses the devices of asides and soliloquies to allow his heroes and, in this case, his "villain," a chance to immediately make clear his intentions and motivations to the audience – as Shylock does here.

Shylock's declaration of his hatred for Antonio immediately intensifies the drama of the scene; the audience now waits to see in what way he will be able to catch Antonio "upon the hip" and "feed fat the ancient grudge I bear him." Then Shylock is called back from the front of the stage by Bassanio, and he pretends to notice Antonio for the first time. Their greeting has ironic overtones for the audience, which has just heard Shylock's opinion of Antonio. There then follows a debate between Antonio and Shylock on the subject of usury, or the taking of interest on a loan – permissible for Shylock but *not* for Antonio, according to Antonio's moral code.

In making Shylock avoid committing himself immediately to lending Antonio the money, Shakespeare is building a dramatic crisis. For example, Antonio's mounting impatience leads to increased arrogance; he compares the moneylender to the "apple rotten at the heart." Still, however, Shylock does not respond; he pretends to muse on the details of the loan, producing from Antonio the curt and insolent remark, "Well, Shylock, shall we be beholding to you?" Only then does Shylock begin to answer directly, and he does so with calculated calm. "Signior Antonio," he says, "many a time and oft/ In the Rialto you have rated me. . . ." His words are controlled but carry a cold menace that silences Antonio at once. At the phrase "You call me misbeliever, cut-throat dog," Shylock reveals to us that Antonio did "void your rheum upon my beard/ And foot me as you spurn a stranger cur/

Over your threshold!" This is a vivid dramatic change, climaxing in his taunting lines: "Hath a dog money? Is it possible/ A cur can lend three thousand ducats?"

In Shylock's earlier aside ("I'll hate him [Antonio] for he is a Christian"), the audience was inclined to pigeonhole Shylock as the "villain" of this drama; anyone who hates a man simply because he is a *Christian* must logically be a villain. Yet now, in this speech, there is much more depth and complexity; we are given a most revealing glimpse of a man who has been a victim, whose imposition of suffering on others is directly related to his *own* suffering. Shakespeare is manipulating us emotionally; we have to reconsider Shylock's character.

After Shylock regains control of himself and skillfully leads Antonio toward the sealing of the bond, he says that he would like to be friends" with Antonio. This gives him the excuse to make light of the bond, but a bond sealed "in merry sport" – a bond where a pound of flesh can "be cut off and taken/ In what part of your body pleaseth me." Here, Shakespeare has the difficult problem of making us believe that Antonio is actually innocent enough to accept such a condition; after all, Antonio is probably fifty years old and a wealthy merchant; he is no schoolboy, and this "merry sport" of a bond is absurd. Clearly, to us, Shylock's interest is not only in money in this case, but Antonio does not realize this, nor does he realize or fully understand the depth of Shylock's hatred of him. He is therefore unable to be persuaded that this bond is dangerous. To him, the bond is merely a "merry bond." And thus Shylock is able to rhetorically ask Bassanio: "Pray you tell me this:/ If he should break his day, what should I gain/ By the exaction of the forfeiture?"

Shakespeare has set up a situation in which a man has put his life in the hands of a moral enemy and the outcome depends on fortune – that is, whether or not Antonio's merchant ships survive pirates and the high seas. Antonio and Shylock are diametrical opposites. Shylock is cunning, cautious, and crafty; he belongs to a race which has been persecuted since its beginnings. As a Christian, Antonio is easy-going, trusting, slightly melancholy, romantic, and naive. Shylock trusts only in the tangible – that is, in the bond. Antonio trusts in the intangible – that is, in luck. Here, Shylock seems almost paranoid and vengeful, but on

24

the other hand, Antonio seems ignorantly over-confident – rather stupid because he is so lacking in common sense.

ACT II – SCENE 1

Summary

There is a flourish of trumpets, and the Prince of Morocco enters. Portia, along with her confidante, Nerissa, and several ladies-in-waiting are present, and the prince, knowing that he is only one of many suitors who seek Portia's hand in marriage, begins his courtship straightforwardly – that is, he initiates the subject of the color of his skin. Being from Morocco, he comes "in the shadowed livery of the burnished sun." He has a very dark complexion, and he begs Portia to "mislike [him] not for [his] complexion." Despite the color of his skin, however, his blood is as red as any of Portia's other suitors, and he is as brave as any of them.

Portia tells him that he is "as fair" as any of the men who have come to seek her "affection." Furthermore, were she not bound by the terms of her father's will, he would stand as good a chance as any other suitor. According to her father's will, however, if the prince wishes to try for her hand, he must take his chances like all the others. If he chooses wrongly, he must remain a bachelor forever; he is "never to speak to lady afterward/ In way of marriage."

The prince is not easily deterred; he is ready for the test. All in good time, says Portia; first, they shall have dinner together. Then his "hazard shall be made." There is a flourish of trumpets, and the two exit.

Commentary

In contrast to the businesslike mood of Act I, this act begins with much visual and verbal pomp. Visually, the Prince of Morocco and Portia enter from opposite sides of the stage to a "flourish of cornets," each followed by a train of attendants. Morocco then opens the dialogue with a proud reference to his dark skin, and the rich, regular, sonorous poetry which Shakespeare gives him to speak suggests that the prince possesses a large, imposing physical presence. Because we have already listened to Portia blithely dismiss the other suitors who have already appeared at Belmont so far, here, her greeting has both courtesy and respect – "Yourself, renowned Prince, then stood as fair/ As any comer I have looked on yet/ For my affection."

Since there are three caskets for Portia's suitors to choose from, there will therefore be three occasions in which suitors will attempt the test of the caskets to win Portia in marriage. Thus the three contestants are subtly contrasted. The first, Morocco, is intensely physical; he is a warrior. He speaks of his red blood, the power of his scimitar, and of the courage that can "mock the lion when 'a roars for prey." Morocco is a straightforward soldier-prince; he is rightly self-assured and is contrasted to the Prince of Arragon (in Scene 9 of this act), whose excessive pride is concerned with lineage and position. Both of these suitors will fail, and although the audience knows, or suspects this (since the play is a romantic comedy, it must end happily, with Bassanio making the right choice and winning Portia), this knowledge does not interfere with the thrill of dramatic anticipation as Morocco, first, and, later, Arragon make their choices. Rationally, we may know *how* a story ends, but this does not prevent our imaginative excitement in watching the unfolding of events.

ACT II – SCENE 2

Summary

After the last, rather serious scene in Belmont, we return to Venice, and the initial emphasis here is on Launcelot Gobbo, Shylock's servant, an "unthrifty knight." Launcelot is debating with himself as to whether or not he should remain in Shylock's service; he is tempted to leave and find employment elsewhere, but he is unable to make up his mind. The decision is difficult, he says, for he feels the weight of his "conscience. . . . hanging about the neck of his heart."

The comedy builds when Launcelot's father, Old Gobbo, comes onstage. Old Gobbo is "more than sandblind" and does not recognize his son. He sees before him only the dim image of a man who he hopes can direct him to Shylock's house. Launcelot is delighted to encounter his father, whom he has not seen for a long time, and so he conceals his true identity and playfully confuses the old man with much clowning and double-talk, before revealing who he really is and kneeling to receive his father's blessing.

Bassanio now enters, along with Leonardo and other followers, and he is enthusiastically talking of preparations for a dinner tonight, complete with a masque, to which he has invited his friends to celebrate his departure for Belmont, where he will begin his courtship of Portia. Launcelot is quick to note Bassanio's good mood, and he immediately speaks to him about Bassanio's hiring him as a servant. Bassanio agrees and orders a new set of livery for his new servant.

Gratiano enters, looking for Bassanio, and tells him, "I must go with you to Belmont." Bassanio is hesitant, but he finally consents, urging Gratiano to modify his "wild behaviour," which Gratiano agrees to do. But he will do that tomorrow. Tonight, he says, shall be a night of merriment, a gala inaugurating his setting out for Belmont.

Commentary

This scene, like Scene 1 and most of the rest of the nine scenes in Act II, deals with minor diversions and developments in the plot — the elopement of Lorenzo and Jessica, and Launcelot Gobbo's transfer of his services from Shylock to Bassanio.

Almost all of this scene is taken up with the antics of Launcelot Gobbo, and it may be useful here to consider for a moment the clowns and comedy of the Elizabethan stage. Two of the most important members of any Elizabethan theatrical company were the actor who played the tragic hero and the actor who played the clown. It is obvious why the actor who played the great tragic roles was important, but it is perhaps not so easy for us to see, from the standpoint of the modern theater, why the role of a clown took on so much importance. The clowns, though, were great favorites with the Elizabethan audiences. Their parts involved a great deal of comic stage business — improvised actions, gestures, and expressions — and they had their own special routines. Launcelot, for example, would be given a great deal of leeway in using his own special comic devices. Much here depends on the actor's "business" – mime, expressions of horror or stupid self-satisfaction, burlesque or parody movements around the stage, and so forth. This sort of scene is not written for *verbal* comedy (as Portia's scenes are); rather, Shakespeare wrote them to give his actors as much scope as was necessary for *visual* antics. Today we call these gimmicks "sight gags" or "slapstick." The dialogue itself is not particularly witty because the comedy was meant to be mostly physical. Launcelot's opening speech takes the form of a debate between "the fiend" and his own "conscience." The comedy here lies in the fact that the jester-clown Launcelot should regard himself as the hero of a religious drama; but this gives him the opportunity to mimic two separate parts, jumping back and forth on the stage and addressing himself: "Well, my conscience says, 'Launcelot, budge not.' 'Budge,' says the fiend. 'Budge not,' says my conscience" (18-20). Visually, this makes for good comedy; while reading this play aloud, one can enhance this brief scene by imagining that the voice of the conscience is delivered in high, falsetto, flute-like tones; the voice of the fiend, in contrast, is delivered in low, evil-sounding growls.

In addition to this clowning business, verbal confusion was also a favorite device in this sort of scene, and it occurs throughout the play. Notice, for example, the directions for finding Shylock's house which Launcelot gives to his father: "Turn up on your right hand at the next turning, but at the next turning of all, on your left; marry, at the very next turning of no hand, but turn down indirectly. . . ." Small wonder that Old Gobbo exclaims, " 'twill be a hard way to hit!"

There is more visual comedy when the two Gobbos confront Bassanio at line 120. Here, it is suggested by the lines that Launcelot bends down behind his father, popping up to interrupt him at every other line and finishing his sentences for him. This kind of comedy depends on visual and verbal confusion, especially mistaking obvious words and phrases. Particularly characteristic of this clowning is the confusion of word meanings. Here, Launcelot speaks of his "true-begotten father," and he uses "infection" for affection, "frutify" for certify, "defect" for effect, and so on.

Toward the close of the scene, two more details of the central plot are developed. First, Launcelot leaves Shylock's household for that of Bassanio; this prepares us for a similar, if a much greater defection from Shylock by his daughter, Jessica, in the following scene. It also makes it possible for Launcelot to appear at Belmont in the final act, where a little of his clowning adds to the general good humor. Second, Gratiano announces his intention of going to Belmont with Bassanio; he must be there to marry Nerissa and take part in the comedy of the "ring story," which ends the play with lighthearted teasing wit.

ACT II – SCENE 3

Summary

In this scene, set in Shylock's house, we are introduced to Jessica, Shylock's daughter. She is speaking with Launcelot, and she expresses her sorrow that he decided to leave his position as her father's servant. "Our house is hell," she says, "and thou a merry devil/ Didst rob it of some taste of tediousness." She then gives him a letter to deliver secretly to her lover Lorenzo "who is thy new master's [Bassanio's] guest." After Launcelot leaves, we discover that Jessica is planning to elope with Lorenzo; in addition, she is planning to renounce her father's faith and become a Christian.

Commentary

This brief scene in Act II provides the final piece of plot exposition. Here, we are introduced to Shylock's daughter, Jessica, and in her first words, we have a clear idea about her relationship with her father, and we receive some justification for her plan to leave the old moneylender's house; she says, "Our house is hell."

Her love letter, to be given to Lorenzo, will figure in the second of the play's love affairs (Gratiano and Nerissa will prove a third in this play). It is important that the audience in this scene and in the next scene be aware of Jessica's elopement with Lorenzo, since it adds very heavy irony to Shylock's multiple warnings to his daughter in Scene 5 to guard his house well.

In this scene, Shylock is cast in the clichéd role of the villain, primarily because of Jessica's remarks, but one should remember that in a romantic comedy, one of the fathers would have to be a villain of sorts; here, it is Shylock. Interestingly, even though Jessica's intention to leave her father's household and rush into her lover's arms seems natural enough, Jessica is aware of her "sin," being her father's child. Finally, though, as part of the romantic plot, all will be well with Jessica, and she will be a part of the general happiness at the play's end.

ACT II – SCENE 4

Summary

Gratiano, Lorenzo, Salarino, and Salanio discuss their plans for Bassanio's dinner party and masque that night. All of the preparations have not been made; for example, one of the things which they have neglected to do, and which must be done, is to hire young boys to act as torchbearers for the evening so that the gala party will be brightly lighted. This is to be a special evening, and all details must be considered.

While they are talking, Launcelot enters, on his way to invite Shylock to the party, and he delivers Jessica's letter to Lorenzo. Lorenzo reads it and sends Jessica a reply: "Tell gentle Jessica/ I will not fail her; speak it privately." Lorenzo then tells his friends that *he* has found a torchbearer, and he confides to Gratiano that Jessica is going to disguise herself as a page tonight and elope with him; furthermore, she will escape with enough gold and jewels for a proper dowry. Lorenzo feels sure that Jessica, in a page's attire, can successfully disguise herself as a torchbearer for Bassanio's party and not be recognized.

Commentary

The masque, which the characters discuss, never occurs; perhaps the play has been cut or perhaps Shakespeare felt that there was simply not enough time for a masque. In any event, however, the anticipation of the masque causes the audience to envision it, and thus it suggests a youthful and romantic background to the Jessica-Lorenzo development ("Fair Jessica shall be my torchbearer"), a mood which is clearly antithetical contrast to the self-denying and puritanical life of Shylock's household.

ACT II – SCENE 5

Summary

Preparing to leave for Bassanio's dinner party, to which he has accepted an invitation, after all, Shylock encounters Launcelot, who has come, of course, to deliver Lorenzo's reply to Jessica. Shylock chides his former servant and says that in Launcelot's new capacity as Bassanio's attendant, Launcelot will no longer be able to "gor-mandize," and "sleep, and snore," as he was (theoretically) able to do with Shylock. All the while that Shylock is expostulating to Launcelot, his speeches are broken with repeated calls for Jessica. When she finally appears, he gives her the keys to the house and tells her that he is going to attend Bassanio's dinner party. Grum-bling, he confesses that he accepted the invitation "in hate, to feed upon/ The prodigal Christian." He elaborates further and says that he is "right loath to go"; he has a foreboding that "some ill [is] a-brewing. . . ."

Launcelot urges his former master to go; he too has a premoni-tion. He has a "feeling" (because his "nose fell a-bleeding on Black Monday last at six o'clock in the morning. . . .") that Bassanio is preparing an elaborate masque as part of the evening's entertain-ment. Shylock is horrified at the suggestion that he may have to en-dure the bawdy, showy heresies of a Christian masque. He insists that if Jessica hears any sounds of the masque, she is to "stop up [his] house's ears," and she herself is to keep inside and not "gaze on Christian fools with varnished faces [painted masks]"; he vows that no "sound of shallow foppery" will enter his "sober house." Despite grave misgivings, Shylock finally decides to set out for Bassanio's dinner party – but not before repeating one final command for Jessica to stay inside: "Fast bind, fast find – / A proverb never stale in thrifty mind." Shylock exits then, not realizing that Launcelot was able to whisper a quick word of advice to Jessica before he left: she is to be on watch for "a Christian" who will be "worth a Jewess' eye" – Lorenzo.

daughter eloping

/ innocent

Alone on the stage, Jessica anticipates her impending elopement and utters a prophetic couplet that closes the scene:

> Farewell; and if my fortune be not crossed,
> I have a father, you a daughter, lost.
>
> (55-56)

Commentary

This scene elaborates on and give additional dimension to the
character of Shylock. We know of Jessica's intended elopement, and
thus we understand Shylock's sense of foreboding when he speaks of
"some ill a-brewing." Indeed, ill is brewing for him, and much of the
drama in this scene is derived from the fact that both Jessica and
Launcelot are anxious to get Shylock on his way so that they can
make final arrangements for the elopement. Their suspense at his in-
decision as to whether to go or stay is the key to the drama here;
Shylock says, "I am bid forth. . . . But wherefore should I go? . . .
But yet I'll go . . . I am right loath to go." Launcelot, in his excitement and anxiety, almost gives the elopement plans away. He lets
slip the phrase "They have conspired together" (line 22), but he immediately covers his mistake with some confused nonsense about
his own prophetic dream; he predicts that there will be a masque at
the party because his "nose fell a-bleeding on Black Monday. . . ."
This is not only a comic parallel of Shylock's superstition concerning
dreams, but also diverts the old moneylender from the suggestion
that his daughter might be planning to elope.

Also central to this scene is Shylock's concern with his possessions; note, for example, his obsession with locking and guarding
the house, which he entrusts to Jessica. He calls her to him and
gives her his keys, then almost takes them back again: "I am loath
to go," he says. The emphasis is on the *protection* of his wealth, and
this emphasis appears again when he says, "Hear you me, Jessica:/
Lock up my doors," and it occurs again in "stop my house's ears – I
mean my casements"; even the idea of *music* entering his house is
repellent to Shylock. He warns Jessica that perhaps he "will return
immediately," thus producing new anxiety in her – and in the emotions of the audience. Shylock's last words – "shut doors after you./
Fast bind, fast find" – illustrate his inability to leave his *possessions.*
Yet, even so, Shakespeare manages to suggest in his portrayal of
Shylock's miserliness, a kind of unspoken, grudging affection for his

daughter and, in this scene, for Launcelot; he calls Jessica, affectionately, "Jessica my girl," and of Launcelot, he says, "the patch [a kindly nickname for a clown] is kind enough." Still, though, both phrases are immediately followed by a return to his central fixation—his possessions. The great irony of the scene, of course, lies in *our* knowledge that while Shylock is concerned with his valuables, it is his *daughter* that he is about to lose, and it is to her that he entrusts his possessions. This is classic dramatic irony.

ACT II – SCENE 6

Summary

Gratiano and Salarino, masked and costumed for Bassanio's party, wait for Lorenzo under the overhanging roof (the "penthouse") of Shylock's house. Gratiano is puzzled that Lorenzo is late for his rendezvous with Jessica; he knows that lovers usually "run before the clock." Lorenzo's delay is certainly uncharacteristic of most young lovers.

Suddenly, Lorenzo rushes onstage, apologizes for his lateness, and calls to Jessica. She appears above, dressed as a boy, and tosses down a casket of money and jewels to Lorenzo. Shyly, she says that she is ashamed to be eloping with her beloved while she is so unbecomingly dressed as a boy. "Cupid himself," she tells Lorenzo, "would blush." Lorenzo tells her that she must play her part well; not only must she successfully be convincing as a boy, but she must also be his torchbearer at Bassanio's party—a fact that unnerves her. The idea of "hold[ing] a candle to [her] shames" is frightening. She is certain that what Lorenzo is asking of her will lead to discovery, and she feels that she "should be obscured." Lorenzo is finally able to reassure her, however, and Jessica turns back to do two last things before they elope. She wants to "make fast the doors" (as her father instructed her to do), and she wants to get "some more ducats."

Gratiano praises her, and Lorenzo reaffirms that he will love her in his "constant soul," for she is "wise, fair, and true." Jessica then enters below, and the lovers and Salarino exit.

Antonio enters and, finding Gratiano, tells him that there will be "no masque tonight." The wind has changed, and Bassanio and his men must sail for Belmont. Gratiano admits that he is relieved that there will be no feasting and no masque. He is anxious to be "under sail and gone tonight."

Commentary

There is no real break between this scene and the preceding one. As Shylock exits, and Jessica exits only moments later, Gratiano and Salarino enter, costumed for the masque and carrying torches. Gratiano, as we might expect, does most of the talking as the two chaps wait beneath the overhanging roof of Shylock's house.

When Lorenzo arrives onstage and Jessica appears above him, a modern audience would almost certainly think of the lovers Romeo and Juliet. Thus the romantic mood is immediately set – except that this romantic heroine is dressed in "the lovely garnish of a boy." This was a popular and recurrent Elizabethan stage convention, and a very convenient one, since all the girls' roles were played by boys. Shakespeare uses this disguise convention later in this same play with Portia and Nerissa disguised as a lawyer and his clerk.

At this point, since Jessica is both deserting her father's house *and* robbing it, it is almost too easy, in one sense, to disapprove of her; Shylock hasn't really shown us a truly villainous side. One doesn't take the "pound of flesh" bond literally – yet.

ACT II – SCENE 7

Summary

At Belmont, in a room in Portia's house, the Prince of Morocco surveys the three caskets – one of gold, one of silver, and one of lead. He must choose one, and if he chooses the correct one, his reward will be the "fair Portia." As he reads the words engraved on the top of each casket, he ponders each of the cryptic inscriptions. On the leaden casket, he reads, "Who chooseth me must give and hazard all he hath"; on the silver casket, he reads, "Who chooseth me shall get as much as he deserves"; and on the golden casket, he reads, "Who chooseth me shall gain what many men desire." Portia informs him that the correct casket contains her picture.

Morocco reviews the inscriptions again and rejects the lead casket as being not worth the high stakes for which he gambles. He ponders a long time over the silver casket. The words "get as much as he deserves" intrigue him. He is quite sure that he *deserves* Portia; he deserves her "in birth," "in fortune," "in grace," "in qualities of breeding," and, most of all, "in love." Yet, ultimately, he rejects the silver casket because he refuses to believe that Portia's father would "immure" a portrait of his treasured daughter in a metal "ten times undervalued [as] tried gold." The prince reasons that a portrait of Portia – a "mortal, breathing saint," a woman whom "all the world desires" – could be only within the golden casket. He chooses, therefore, the golden casket, hoping to find "an angel in a golden bed."

When he unlocks the casket and looks inside, he discovers only a skull ("carrion Death") and a scroll rolled up and inserted within the skull's "empty eye." He takes it out and reads the message: "All that glisters is not gold; . . . Gilded tombs do worms infold." Defeated and grieving, he makes a hasty exit with his entourage. "A gentle riddance," comments Portia.

Commentary

In contrast to the scene preceding this one, now we have another colorful and theatrical spectacle of yet another rich suitor who has come to try and outwit fortune and claim Portia for his bride.

As Morocco inspects the caskets, Shakespeare is able to inform the audience more fully of the details of the casket competition for Portia's hand. The casket that will win her contains a miniature portrait of her, and all of the caskets have inscriptions upon them, which Morocco reads for us. These inscriptions are important; each succeeding suitor will reflect upon them, and as he does so, he will reveal the truth about his own character. The inscriptions are, of course, intentionally ambiguous; they can be interpreted in more than one way. Remembering that this is a romantic comedy, we expect that Morocco will misinterpret them, as will Arragon later, and that finally Bassanio will read the inscriptions and interpret them correctly.

We should remember as we read this scene that Portia herself, at this point, does not know which of the caskets will win her. As

Morocco moves from one to the next, Portia will be reacting on stage, silently revealing her thoughts, for she cannot guide Morocco, and we have some evidence for believing that Portia is not usually a quiet woman.

Morocco's long speech, beginning at line 13, was no doubt inserted by Shakespeare to allow the actor plenty of time to move back and forth with much hesitation between the caskets. Talking to himself, he says, "Pause there, Morocco. . . . What if I strayed no further, but chose here?" He is postponing the moment of choice and prolonging the suspense of this dramatic moment. We have already seen Morocco and know that he is a proud and powerful prince, rich in his dress and in his language, and therefore it is no surprise to watch him move from the *least* beautiful and outwardly appealing of the caskets to the *most* beautiful; he has, he says, "a golden mind." Thus he makes the most straightforward and obvious choice – for him: the golden casket, for "Never so rich a gem/ Was set in worse than gold." When he opens it and finds the skull and the scroll, Shakespeare's moral is clear – that is, wealth and sensory beauty, symbolized here by gold, are merely transitory: "Many a man his life hath sold/ But my outside to behold." We shall see later that the test of the caskets contains a theme that occurs elsewhere in the play: the difference between what merely *seems* and what really *is* – that is, the difference between appearance and reality. The caskets also suggest another element in the play – namely, the illusion that material wealth (gold and silver) is of value, when, in reality, it is of ultimately little value. Yet material wealth is Shylock's obsession; gold is his real god, and therein is his tragic flaw.

ACT II – SCENE 8

Summary

Salarino and Salanio discuss developments in Venice. When Shylock discovered that Jessica was gone, he demanded that the Duke of Venice have Bassanio's ship searched; this proved to be impossible because Bassanio had already sailed. Antonio, however, assured the Duke that Lorenzo and Jessica were *not* on board Bassanio's ship. Salanio then describes how Shylock raved in the

streets, crying, "My daughter! O my ducats! O my daughter!/ Fled
with a Christian," while "all the boys in Venice" followed him, mock-
ing him, his daughter, and his ducats.

Salanio worries about what will happen to Antonio; he knows
Shylock's temper. Jessica's elopement and Antonio's swearing that
Bassanio had no part in her escape "bade no good" for Antonio. He
knows that Antonio *must* "keep his day" (repay his debt when it
comes due) or else "he shall pay for this." Salanio is likewise worried
about Antonio's future. Only yesterday, a Frenchman told him
about an Italian ship that had sunk in the English Channel. He immediately thought of Antonio, hoping that the ship was not one of
his. The news about the shipwreck must be broken gently to Antonio because Antonio is a sensitive man. Realizing that Antonio
may need cheering up, Salanio and Salarino decide to pay him a
visit.

Commentary

Salarino's and Salanio's opening lines are hurried and excited.
Here and elsewhere in the play, notably in Act I, Scene 1, these two
act more or less like a chorus; that is to say, they discuss developments of the plot not shown on the stage so that the audience will be
aware of them and also of their importance. Here, they are concerned about Antonio's fate, since Shylock is in a terrible temper, and
the once "merry bond" is no longer "merry."

Salanio's speech, beginning at line 12, is introduced here for two
reasons: First, Shylock's rage must be described *before* it is shown
so that we can anticipate his state of mind at his next entrance. Second, Shylock's loss of both his daughter and much of his money are
important for our understanding the extent of Shylock's desire for
revenge. At the beginning of the play, he has only two real reasons
for hating Antonio – a commercial hatred and a religious hatred. To
these is now added a shattering personal loss – he has lost his
daughter, his only child, to a Christian, a friend of Antonio – making
plausible his implacable desire for revenge against *all* Venetian
Christians in the person of a man whom he has legally cornered: Antonio. In a very real sense, our sympathy goes out to Shylock, yet
Shakespeare keeps us from pitying the man by having Salanio enact
a sort of exaggerated parody of Shylock's greedy, histrionic behavior

as he tells his friend Salarino how Shylock was chased in the streets by young boys, howling after him. Shylock's repetitions of "O my ducats! O my daughter! . . . my ducats and my daughter. . . ." indicate that Jessica is simply, at this point, another possession, like his coins. Thus we are prevented from being too oversympathetic to an obsession which has blinded the old moneylender to the true difference between monetary and human values.

ACT II – SCENE 9

Summary

At Belmont, the Prince of Arragon has arrived to try his luck at choosing the correct casket, and before he decides on one, he promises Portia that he will abide by her father's rules. First, if he fails to choose the casket containing her portrait, he will never reveal which casket he chose; second, he promises never to court another woman; and last, he will leave Belmont immediately.

Reviewing the inscriptions, he rejects the lead casket immediately because he thinks that it is not beautiful enough to give and risk all his possessions for. He also rejects the gold casket because "what many men desire" may place him on the same level with "the barbarous multitudes." He thus chooses the silver casket, which bears the inscription, "Who chooseth me shall get as much as he deserves." Arragon reviews his worth and decides that he "will assume desert" – that is, he feels that he rightfully deserves Portia. When he opens the silver casket, he finds within "the portrait of a blinking idiot" – a picture of a fool's head. He protests the contents; he chose according to what he felt that he deserved: "Did I deserve no more than a fool's head?" Portia reminds him that no man is permitted to judge his own cause. The scroll in the silver casket reads, "There be fools alive, I wis [know],/ Silver'd o'er; and so was this." Arragon departs then with his followers, promising to keep his oath.

Portia is clearly relieved and sums up the reason for the prince's failure: "O, these deliberate fools! When they do choose,/ They have their wisdom by their wit to lose." In other words, even fools choose deliberately and believe that they are wise to deliberate; in fact, it is their excessive deliberation which ultimately defeats them.

A servant announces the arrival of a Venetian ambassador from another suitor and adds that he brings gifts; in fact, in the messenger's estimation, the man who accompanies this latest suitor is "so likely an ambassador of love" that "a day in April never came so sweet." Portia is neither impressed nor optimistic, yet she urges Nerissa to bring the man to her so that she can see for herself this "quick Cupid's post [messenger] that comes so mannerly." Nerissa sighs; "Lord Love," she prays, "if thy will it be," let this suitor be Bassanio!

Commentary

This scene focuses on the Prince of Arragon's choice of the three caskets. The Prince of Morocco's choice was straightforward and simple. He chose the gold casket; it seemed to be the most obvious, most desirable choice. In contrast, the Prince of Arragon's choice is done with more prudence. The prince is a proud man; he seems older than Morocco and almost bloodless, compared to Morocco's fiery charismatic bearing. Often, Shakespeare makes his characters' names suggest their primary qualities; here, "Arragon" was probably chosen for its resemblance to "arrogant." At any rate, Arragon is arrogant, a temperament befitting a Spanish grandee of noble blood, a familiar and conventional figure on the Elizabethan stage.

Once again, we hear the ambiguous inscriptions read for us, and we ourselves puzzle over the enigma of the metals and their relationship to the inscriptions. Arragon considers the caskets, but he does not make Morocco's obvious choice. If gold represents "what many men desire," then Arragon's powerful belief in his own *superiority* to "the fool multitude that choose by show" makes him reject it. We can agree with that logic, but we have to reject his reasoning ultimately because it is based on his absolute assumption of his own superiority to the multitude.

The silver inscription, "Who chooseth me shall get as much as he deserves," has an immediate appeal for Arragon. It prompts his observations on "merit" (lines 35-48), in which he laments the fact that there is so much "undeserved dignity" in the world; he means those who are given honor without coming by it legitimately, through the "true seed" of noble inheritance. The man is a snob; he has absolutely no doubts about what *he* deserves, and since his nobility is inherited nobility, he can safely (he thinks) choose the silver casket and "assume desert."

A factor that we should be aware of in this entire scene is an absence of any evidence that Arragon has any love, or even any affection, for Portia. Portia is "deserved." Nowhere can we discern even an inkling of any craving for her. As was noted, the prince is rather bloodless.

In the suitors' choice of the caskets, we have yet another variation of the illusion-reality theme: gold and silver *appear* to be the obvious choices to the first two suitors, whose motives for choosing are in some way flawed; neither of them is truly in love with Portia, for example. Yet Bassanio, who does love Portia, will choose the casket which *appears* to be the least valuable; in reality, it will turn out to be the most valuable. Thus the ability to choose and to distinguish between what appears to be valuable and what really is valuable depends not so much on intelligence—Shylock is far more intelligent than Antonio or Bassanio—but on something deeper and more intangible. In this play, that certain intangible something is love; it is not glory (Morocco), nor nobility of social position (Arragon), nor wealth (Shylock), but love for another human being, which Bassanio and Portia clearly offer to one another.

At this point, the love plot in the play becomes very much like a fairy tale—the beautiful princess is won by love—not by wealth or rank or by calculation; we are reminded of Nerissa's comment in Act I, Scene 2: the proper casket will "never be chosen by any rightly but one who you shall rightly love." We now know which casket is the right one, and thus we can relax and enjoy the drama of Bassanio's momentous choice. His approach (preceded by "an ambassador of love") is now announced by a messenger, and the fulfillment of the play's love story is clearly anticipated in Nerissa's comment: "A day in April never came so sweet/ To show how costly summer was at hand."

ACT III–SCENE 1

Summary

In Venice, Salanio and Salarino are discussing the latest "news on the Rialto," the bridge in Venice where many business offices are located. There is a rumor that a ship of Antonio's has been wrecked off the southeast coast of England. Salanio despairs – twice – once because of Antonio's bad luck and second, because he sees Shylock approaching. Shylock lashes out at both men, accusing them of being accessories to Jessica's elopement. They expected as much and mock the moneylender, scoffing at his metaphor when he complains that his "flesh and blood" has rebelled. Jessica, they say, is no more like Shylock than ivory is to jet, or Rhenish wine is to red wine. Shylock then reminds the two that their friend Antonio had best "look to his bond. . . . look to his bond." The implication is clear; Shylock has heard of the shipwreck.

Surely, says Salarino, if Antonio forfeits the bond, "thou wilt not take his flesh." Shylock assures them that he *will*, for he is determined to be revenged on Antonio for *many* grievances, all committed against Shylock for one reason: because Shylock is a Jew. A Jew is a human being the same as a Christian, Shylock continues; like a Christian, a Jew has "eyes . . . hands, organs, dimensions, senses, affections, passions . . . [is] hurt . . . subject to the same diseases, [and] healed by the same means. . . ." Like a Christian, a Jew bleeds if pricked, and since a Christian always revenges any wrong received from a Jew, Shylock will follow this example. A servant enters then and informs Salanio and Salarino that Antonio wishes to see them at his house.

As they depart, Shylock's friend Tubal enters. Tubal has traced Jessica to Genoa, where he has heard news of her but could not find her. Shylock again moans about his losses, especially about his diamonds and ducats; he wishes Jessica were dead. Tubal interrupts and tells Shylock that he picked up additional news in Genoa: another of Antonio's ships has been "cast away, coming from Tripolis." Shylock is elated. But as Tubal returns to the subject of Jessica's excessive expenditures in Genoa, Shylock groans again. Thus Tubal reminds Shylock of Antonio's tragic misfortunes, and the moneylender exults once more. One thing is certain, Tubal assures Shylock: "Antonio is certainly undone." Shylock agrees and instructs Tubal to pay a police sergeant in advance to arrest Antonio if he forfeits the bond.

Commentary

This act opens with Salanio and Salarino again functioning as a chorus, informing the audience of the development of events against which the action of the scene will take place. The suggestion made earlier that Antonio's mercantile ventures at sea might founder is now made specific. One of Antonio's ships lies "wracked on the narrow seas . . . where the carcases of many a tall ship lie buried." The news of the danger to Antonio also prepares us for the entrance of Shylock, the embodiment of that danger, who has by now discovered Jessica's elopement.

The moneylender enters, and both we and Salanio know perfectly well "what news" concerns Shylock; Salanio's sardonic greeting, with its pretense of wanting to know "the news," is calculated to infuriate Shylock, for even though we have not seen Shylock since the elopement of his daughter, we know that his anger will have been fueled by the fact that Lorenzo – and, by implication, the whole Christian community – has dealt him a blow. One should be fully aware that Shylock is ever conscious of his Jewishness in a Christian community. Then at the mention of Antonio, Shylock says ominously, "Let him look to his bond." Without question, the bond is "merry" no longer – but Salanio has not comprehended this yet. His half-serious question "Thou wilt not take his flesh. What's that good for?" is answered savagely: "If it will feed nothing else, it will feed my revenge," Shylock declares.

The malicious digs of Salanio and Salarino produce one of Shylock's most dramatic speeches in the play. It is written in prose, but it is a good example of the superb intensity to which Shakespeare can raise mere prose. Shylock's series of accusing, rhetorical questions which form the central portion of the speech, from "Hath not a Jew eyes?" to "If you poison us, do we not die?" completely silences Shylock's tormentors. In fact, this speech silences us. We ourselves have to ponder it. It is one of the greatest pleas for human tolerance in the whole of dramatic literature. But it is also something more, and we must not lose sight of its dramatic importance. It is a prelude to Shylock's final decision concerning how he will deal with Antonio.

Shylock speaks of a Christian's "humility" with heavy sarcasm; "humility," he says, is a much-talked-of Christian virtue, but a virtue which is not much in evidence. The "humility" of a Christian, Shylock says, ceases when a Christian is harmed, for then the Christian takes revenge. That is the Christian's solution, and that will also be Shylock's course of action, his solution to the wrongs he has suffered: "The villainy you teach me I will execute." And toward the end of the speech, he repeats, like a refrain, the word "revenge."

Shylock's speech on revenge is so powerful and so unanswerable that it is lost on Salanio and Salarino, who are none too bright anyway, but their silence on stage stuns us. Shakespeare has manipulated our sympathy. Then, just when we were secure in feeling that Shylock's reasoning was just, Shakespeare shows us another facet of Shylock, one which we have seen before – his concern with possessions – and thus we must reconsider the whole matter of justice which we thought we had just solved. Shylock's friend Tubal enters and in the exchange which follows, we realize that Shylock has become a miser in order to build his own personal defense against the hostile Christian mercantile world of Venice. But his defense has increased to such an extent that he no longer can contain it; it possesses him now. He cannot properly distinguish between the love of riches and the love for a human being – his love for his daughter, Jessica. Shylock's obsession for possessing has blinded him; his anger at the Christian world has corrupted even his love for his daughter: "I would my daughter were dead at my foot, and the jewels in her ear! Would she were hearsed at my foot, and the ducats in her coffin!" Thereby, we see the extent of Shylock's hatred. By the end of the scene, the audience is convinced, if it was not before, that Shylock's attack on Antonio will be absolutely relentless. If he can, he will literally take his "pound of flesh."

ACT III – SCENE 2

Summary

At Belmont, Portia would like Bassanio to delay before he chooses one of the caskets. Already she has fallen in love with him, and she fears the outcome. She asks him to "tarry," to "pause a day or two," to "forbear awhile"; anything, she tells him, to keep him from possibly choosing the wrong casket. Bassanio, however, begs to choose one of them. His anxiety is too great. If he waits, it is as though he "lives on the rack." Thus Portia acquiesces and tells her servants that this choice is no ordinary choice; therefore, she would like music to be played "while he doth make his choice."

The song which is sung, beginning "Tell me where is fancy bred," has ominous lyrics. Bassanio surveys the caskets, reads their inscriptions, and is reminded by the background music that "fancy" is sometimes bred in the heart and is sometimes bred in the head. The words seem to warn him not to judge by external appearance. Consequently, Bassanio rejects the golden casket; it is a symbol for all "outward shows"; likewise, he rejects the silver casket, calling it a "common drudge/ 'Tween man and man." Instead, he chooses the casket made of "meagre lead," which is the least attractive of the caskets — if they are judged by appearance alone.

When Bassanio's choice is made, Portia prays in an aside for help in containing her emotions. She watches rapturously as Bassanio opens the lead casket and finds in it a picture of Portia, which, though beautifully painted, fails to do her justice, in Bassanio's opinion. Alongside Portia's portrait, there is a scroll which tells him, "Turn you where your lady is/ And claim her with a loving kiss." Still giddy from his success, Bassanio does so, and Portia, who only a moment before was mistress of herself and of all her possessions, now commits herself and all she owns to her new lord. She also presents him with a ring, a symbol of their union, which he is never to "part from, lose, or give away." Bassanio promises to wear the ring as long as he lives.

Nerissa and Gratiano congratulate the lovers and announce that they also have made a match and ask permission to be married at the wedding ceremony of Portia and Bassanio. Portia agrees to the double wedding, and Gratiano boastfully wagers that he and Nerissa produce a boy before they do.

While the lovers are enjoying their happiness, Lorenzo, Jessica, and Salerio arrive. Salerio says that he has come with a letter from Antonio to Bassanio, and that he met Lorenzo and Jessica, whom he persuaded to come with him. As Portia welcomes her fiancé's old friends, Bassanio opens Antonio's letter. He reads it, and Portia notices that he has turned pale; the letter contains bad news. She begs him to share the cause of his anguish, and he tells her that he has just read "the unpleasant'st words/ That ever blotted paper." He confesses that he is deeply in debt to "a dear friend" who in turn is in debt to a dangerous enemy. Turning to Salerio, Bassanio asks, "But is it true? . . . Hath all his ventures fail'd?" Has not a single one of Antonio's ships returned safely? Not one, Salerio replies, and be-

44

sides, even if Antonio now had the money to repay Shylock it would do no good, for Shylock is already boasting of how he will demand "justice" and the payment of the penalty for the forfeited bond. Jessica testifies to her father's determination to "have Antonio's flesh" rather than accept "twenty times the value of the sum" that Antonio owes.

When Portia understands that it is Bassanio's "dear friend that is thus in trouble," she offers to pay any amount to prevent his suffering "through Bassanio's fault." But first, she and Bassanio will be married and then immediately afterwards he must go to Antonio's aid, "for never shall you lie by Portia's side/ With an unquiet soul." In Bassanio's absence, she and Nerissa "will live as maids and widows." Bassanio then reads to Portia the full contents of Antonio's letter. Antonio says that he wishes only to see Bassanio before he dies; his plans "have all miscarried," he says; his "creditors grow cruel"; his "estate is very low"; and his "bond to the Jew is forfeit." Yet, Antonio says, all debts between him and Bassanio are "cleared," and he says that he wishes only "that I might but see you at my death." Portia comprehends the gravity of the situation. Bassanio must leave at once. "O love, dispatch all business, and be gone!" she tells him, as her newly bethrothed lover makes ready to leave for Venice.

Commentary

This long scene brings the casket story to its climax with Bassanio's choice. It begins with Portia's speech begging Bassanio to delay in making his choice of caskets, "for in choosing wrong/ I lose your company." Essentially, this speech is evidence for us of Portia's love for Bassanio, and the charm of her speech lies in the fact that Portia cannot openly admit her love. She continues, and her attempts to verbally circumvent stating outright her feelings for Bassanio lead her to utter absolute nonsense. She declares: "One half of me is yours, the other half yours−/ Mine own I would say; but if mine, then yours,/ And so all yours!" This makes absolutely no sense at all; she is nearly giving in to her urge to tell Bassanio directly of her love for him.

Bassanio is obviously relieved to see that his love is returned. He speaks of feeling as though he were strained tautly on the rack. This admission, in turn, relieves Portia's anxiety somewhat, and her old spirit of jesting returns and she wittily picks up on Bassanio's choice of metaphor and teases him. This witty wordplay has the effect of delaying the choice of caskets and further allowing Portia to relax and display her spirit and sense of wit. We are never allowed to forget her intelligence because this element will be the key ingredient in the play's climactic scene. Bassanio moves to the caskets, and Portia begins a lovely speech, built around the notion of sacrifice. Her phrase "I stand for sacrifice" is particularly apt. Twice, we have watched Portia prepare to become a sort of sacrificial victim, as it were, to unwanted suitors. She has not complained, but we now see that her role in this casket contest contains special intensity. Should Bassanio choose wrongly, she will literally be a sacrifice to a later, unloved husband, as well as being forever a victim of unfulfilled love.

The central idea in the song that is used as background music while Bassanio is making his choice of caskets focuses on the word "fancy." Fancy, for Elizabethans, carried the meaning of whimsical affection. Bassanio picks up on this idea and elaborates on it when he meditates on the way in which "outward shows" mislead or deceive the observer. He extends this perception to law, religion, military honor, and physical beauty.

We are thus reminded of the way in which the Princes of Morocco and Arragon were taken in by the outer *appearance* of the gold and silver caskets. Bassanio rejects both of these caskets, and his reasons are significant in the total meaning of the play. He calls gold "hard food for Midas"; Midas imagined that gold itself could be something nutritive or lifegiving, and he starved to death for his mistake. This causes us to think of the play's Midas-figure—Shylock, for whom wealth is, in itself, something of final, ultimate value. Bassanio calls silver the "common drudge/ 'Tween man and man." Although silver is valued as a precious metal, more often than not it is a medium of exchange—money—and again, we think of Shylock's misplaced values, which make *silver* an end in itself. And so Bassanio finally comes to choose the least likely looking casket—the leaden one—and, of course, his choice is the right one.

Both Bassanio's speech and his choice of caskets touch on one of the central themes of the play—the contrast between appearance and reality; what appears to be valuable (gold and silver) turns out to be worthless, and what appears to be worthless (lead) turns out to be valuable. If we ask ourselves why Bassanio is enabled to judge rightly when others fail, the answer is simply that his motive is love, rather than pride or the desire for worldly gain.

Another idea that Shakespeare is developing here is concerned, again, with wealth. Bassanio sees wealth as useful only in securing love and happiness. Bassanio's conduct suggests that the only use for wealth, for "all that he hath," is in giving or risking it in the pursuit of happiness, not in hoarding it or worshipping it for its own sake.

The exchange of vows between Portia and Bassanio is conducted at an intense and exalted level. But because the play is a romantic comedy, its tone becomes lighter when Gratiano reveals that now that Bassanio has won Portia, *he* has won Nerissa, and his wooing is presented in bold contrast to Bassanio. Gratiano has worked at it "until I sweat again," and he offers to bet that he and Nerissa will be the first of the two couples to produce a child, which rounds off the whole sequence with a typical coarse jest. The Elizabethans would have loved this ribald touch. Portia and Bassanio have presented their idyllic romantic love as something ideal; Gratiano readjusts the balance by the reminder that love is a physical as well as a spiritual union. So far, Venice and Belmont—the world of mercantile ventures and the world of love—have been kept separate. Now, with the arrival of Lorenzo, Jessica, and Salerino from Venice, these two worlds meet, and the evils of wealth, spawned in Venice, disrupt the happy serenity of Belmont. The news of Antonio's danger puts a fearful obstacle in the way of the fulfillment of the play's love story—for now Bassanio is torn by an agonizing conflict between his love and loyalty toward his new wife and his love and loyalty to his old friend Antonio.

Indicative of Portia's rare character in this scene is her immediate reaction to the crisis at hand. She makes a decision and immediately attempts to put it into effect. Bassanio, she says, must "First go with me to church and call me wife,/ And then away to Venice to your friend!" With such decisive ingenuity, it comes as no real surprise to us later when she is able to both conceive and successfully execute the strategy of the lawyer's disguise and the courtroom victory over Shylock.

Summary

In Venice, Antonio has been allowed to leave the jail, accompanied by his jailer. He hopes to speak with Shylock and plead for mercy, but Shylock refuses to listen. Five times while Antonio begs Shylock to let him speak, the moneylender repeats emphatically, "I'll have my bond!" Antonio has publicly called Shylock a "dog"; now Antonio will feel the fangs of that dog. Shylock refuses to be a "soft and dull-eyed fool" and "rent, sigh, and yield." He is absolutely certain that the Duke of Venice will see that justice is carried out according to the terms of the bargain.

Salarino tries to comfort Antonio, but is unsuccessful. Antonio knows that one of the chief reasons why Shylock hates him so much is that Antonio often saved people who were in debt to Shylock by paying their debts for them. Thus he prevented Shylock from foreclosing and claiming their collateral. He also knows that the Duke of Venice must judge according to the letter of the law. Venice is an international trade center; moneylending is a major business and cannot be treated lightly. Antonio must pay his debt according to his contract. He knows that Shylock seeks his life, and the law cannot save him. He is prepared to die if only Bassanio will "come/ To see me pay his debt, and then I care not."

Commentary

In this short scene, the action of the bond plot quickens toward its climax at the beginning of Act IV. Here, Shylock's language indicates his obsession with a single idea through the repetition of a single word. The word is "bond," repeated twice at the opening of his speech, recurring again at lines 12 and 13, and a final time as Shylock makes his exit, deaf to any more pleading: "I will have my bond."

In stark contrast to Shylock's fiery outbursts is Antonio's quiet, almost fatalistic acceptance of his position. He sees that prayers are useless; later, he conceives of himself as being a "tainted wether of

48

the flock." The phrase "He seeks my life" is delivered with the hopeless finality of one already on the way to execution. Such passive acceptance suggests that he is doomed and increases our dramatic anticipation of what is to come. Furthermore, Antonio himself points out that the Venetian state cannot save him; their commercial existence depends upon the rigorous enforcement of the law. Yet, Shakespeare has embedded in our minds how miserly Shylock is; now he teases us and keeps us in suspense: will Portia's money be enough to satisfy Shylock and make him give up his obsession with the "bond" of a pound of flesh?

ACT III – SCENE 4

Summary

At Belmont, following the departure of Bassanio, Lorenzo commends Portia for her perfect understanding of the friendship between her husband and Antonio. Portia says that she feels that if Antonio is worthy of Bassanio's friendship, he is well worth rescuing from "hellish cruelty" at any cost. Leaving the management of her affairs to Lorenzo, she announces that she and Nerissa will go to "a monastery two miles off" until their husbands return. She asks Lorenzo not to deny them this "imposition" and thanks him for agreeing to manage her household until she and Bassanio return. Lorenzo agrees not to interfere, and he and Jessica wish her "all heart's content" and withdraw.

Portia then sends her servant Balthasar "in speed" with a letter to her cousin, the lawyer Doctor Bellario, in Padua, with instructions to bring her "what notes and garments he doth give thee." She tells Nerissa that they will "see [their] husbands/ Before they think of [them]." She then explains her plan for both of them to disguise themselves as young men and follow Bassanio and Gratiano to Venice. Moreover, Portia is so sure that her plan will work that she is willing to bet that she will act the part more convincingly – with "manly stride" and "bragging" – than Nerissa. Her plan *must* succeed; if Bassanio has weighty troubles, then she shares them. Their "souls do bear the equal yoke of love."

Commentary

Lorenzo's praise of Portia, of her nobility and "godlike amity," is introduced here so that she can be associated with Antonio, who is termed the "bosom lover" of Bassanio. Both people are very alike and both of them are very dear to Bassanio. Earlier in the play, it had been Antonio who exemplified the principle of selfless generosity in his treatment of Bassanio. Now Portia takes over this role. Her material generosity to Bassanio symbolizes her loving generosity to him. In contrast to this generosity of both Portia and Antonio is, of course, the character of Shylock. His love has turned inward on himself and on his possessions.

The concepts of friendship and love provided many of the central themes for many Elizabethan plays. For the Elizabethans, friendship was as precious and important a relationship as love. Shakespeare has Portia make it plain that she understands the depth of friendship between Antonio and her husband, and that she is "purchasing the semblance of my soul" in saving Antonio, who is valuable to her because of his friendship with Bassanio. In this scene, Shakespeare also prepares us for Portia's appearance in the court. Under cover of living "in prayer and contemplation," she and Nerissa plan to go to Venice, but this must be kept secret from the other characters of the play.

Again we recognize the capable and audacious woman who is combined with the romantic heroine. She and Nerissa will be "accoutered like young men." This "disguise theme" adds to the comedy, and throughout the trial scene of the play, when Antonio's life hangs in the balance, Shakespeare needs to remind the audience again that what they are watching is, finally, a comedy. We anticipate seeing how well disguised they will be and how well they pull this bit of mischief off. We have seen Portia as the romantic lover and as the wise and witty well-bred woman; now we see her as a woman of the world.

ACT III – SCENE 5

Summary

In a garden at Belmont, the jester Launcelot is teasing Jessica that he fears that she is damned because she is a Jew ("the sins of the father are to be laid on the children"), but she reminds Launcelot that her husband Lorenzo has made her a Christian by marrying her. "The more to blame he," Launcelot jokes: "This making of Christians will raise the price of hogs."

Lorenzo joins them then and pretends jealousy on finding his wife alone with Launcelot. He orders Launcelot to go inside and "bid them prepare for dinner." He suddenly turns to Jessica then and asks her, "How dost thou like the Lord Bassanio's wife?" Jessica praises Portia as being without equal on earth. Lorenzo jokingly responds, "Even such a husband/ Hast thou of me as she is for a wife." Jessica is ready to comment to his teasing when he urges her to save her comments "for table-talk." So with loving jests, they go in to dinner.

Commentary

As in the previous scene, the light comic and romantic relief in this scene is dramatically in order, since it will be immediately followed by the courtroom scene, which is the longest scene in the play and certainly the most emotional scene in the play.

Much of this scene focuses on Launcelot Gobbo's clowning and punning. For example, Launcelot uses "bastard" in a sense that can be both figurative and literal; in addition, he plays elaborately on the two senses of the word "cover" — laying a table and putting on one's hat.

The tender, affectionate exchange between Lorenzo and Jessica at the end of the scene serves to establish their new happiness. They will reappear in Act V in the same roles. In both scenes, we see a Jessica who has changed and blossomed in the environment of Belmont, and this has its significance. Portia and Nerissa are, for example, "to the manner born," but Jessica is an outsider. She was reared by a miser and a man who keenly felt his alienation in the Venetian community. Jessica's character and personality were molded by these attitudes. Now we see her maturing, and her new happiness suggests that Belmont (symbolically, a beautiful mountain) is not so much a place as a state of mind. Jessica's journey from Shylock's dour household to the sunlight and freedom of Belmont is, in its way, a symbolic journey — one from hatred to love and, especially in Jessica's case, a journey from sterility to fruition.

ACT IV – SCENE 1

Summary

The trial of Antonio in a Venetian court of justice begins. The Duke of Venice warns Antonio, the defendant, that the plaintiff (Shylock) is "a stony adversary . . . uncapable of pity . . . [and] void . . . of mercy." Antonio declares that he is ready to suffer quietly. He knows that "no lawful means" can save him now. Shylock is called then, and when he enters, the Duke says that everyone – "the world thinks, and I think so too" – thinks that he should relent at the last moment and spare Antonio, taking "pity on his losses." But Shylock is adamant; he prefers the penalty of a pound of flesh to repayment of three thousand ducats. Why? "Say," says Shylock, "it is my humor." In other words, Shylock wants the pound of flesh for no rational reason. He wants it only because of "a lodged hate and a certain loathing" for Antonio.

Bassanio then tries to reason with Shylock – but without success. Antonio tells Bassanio that he is wasting his time. He himself asks for no further pleas; he begs that judgment be quickly given. Bassanio cannot believe that his friend is serious. He offers *six* thousand ducats, but Shylock refuses. The Duke then asks Shylock a question: "How shalt thou hope for mercy, rendering none?" In reply, Shylock cites the mistreatment of many Venetian slaves by the Venetians themselves, justified by the fact that they *bought* the slaves and can treat them as they please; likewise, the pound of flesh which he has "dearly bought" belongs to him, and he can do with it as he pleases. He therefore demands an immediate judgment confirming this right.

The Duke declares that he is waiting for a certain "Bellario, a learned doctor," to arrive from Padua before he makes a final decision concerning this case. This matter is too weighty for one man to render a single opinion on; therefore, Shylock's demand for judgment will have to wait, and he will have to cease his *demand* – or else the Duke "may dismiss this court."

Bassanio meanwhile tries to cheer up Antonio, vowing that he himself shall give Shylock his own life in place of Antonio's "ere [Antonio] shalt loose for me one drop of blood." Antonio, however, is without hope. He tells Bassanio to "live still, and write mine [Antonio's] epitaph."

At that moment, Nerissa enters the courtroom, dressed like a lawyer's clerk, and delivers a letter from Bellario to the Duke. While the Duke reads the letter, Shylock whets his knife on the sole of his shoe to the horror of Antonio's friends. The clerk of the court then reads aloud the letter from Bellario. The Doctor is ill, but he has sent in his place "a young doctor of Rome," named Balthasar, whose wisdom in the law belies his youth. Bellario says that he never knew "so young a body with so old a head," and he asks the Duke for his "gracious acceptance" of Balthasar in Bellario's stead.

The Duke welcomes young Balthasar, who is, of course, Portia "dressed like a Doctor of Laws." Portia acknowledges that she is familiar with this case and its "strange nature," and she is equally acquainted with the integrity of Venetian law. She asks Antonio if his bond is a valid one, and he admits that it is. She then tells him that Shylock must be merciful. At this, Shylock is shocked: why should *he* be merciful? Because, Portia answers, "mercy is . . . [like] the gentle rain from heaven"; mercy is "twice blest;/ It blesseth him that gives and him that takes." She continues and says that mercy is an attribute of God. It is freely bestowed to temper justice, and those who grant mercy ennoble themselves, especially those people who have the power to dispense punishment and yet award mercy instead. She points out to Shylock that all people "pray for mercy" and "that same prayer" should teach us all to "render the deeds of mercy."

Her speech is lost on Shylock. He "crave[s] the law" and "the penalty and forfeit of [his] bond." He does not care that Bassanio has offered him "thrice the sum" of the bond or even "ten times o'er"; Shylock demands the penalty. Portia pronounces that Venetian law is indeed binding, and whenever decrees are established, alterations set a precedent and "many an error" has been the result. Thus, Antonio's bond is legal, and Shylock can collect the pound of flesh.

Shylock hails the wisdom of this young judge, calling him "noble," "excellent," "wise and upright." He then produces the scales on which he will weigh the flesh; but he balks at Portia's suggestion that he himself personally pay a physician to attend Antonio to see that he does not bleed to death. A judgment is a judgment, and nothing in Antonio's bond mentioned Shylock's hiring a physician. Antonio then turns to Bassanio, bids him farewell, and asks to be commended to Bassanio's "honorable wife," for whose cause the loan was arranged in the first place. He tells Bassanio to tell Portia that he, Antonio, loves Bassanio; Bassanio loses only a friend who loves him dearly. This is all, and "if the Jew do cut but deep enough," death will come quickly. Both Bassanio and Gratiano assure Antonio that they would sacrifice *everything* they have—even their wives—to save him. Both Portia and Nerissa—the Doctor of Law and her clerk of law—comment on this; they doubt that the wives of these loyal friends would "give little thanks" for *that* offer.

Impatient to proceed, Shylock makes ready to begin, but before he can carry out the sentence, Portia stops him. "There is something else," she says. Shylock is legally entitled to take a pound of Antonio's flesh—but no more. That is, Shylock may not take even a single "jot of blood." She then gives Shylock leave to begin his surgery, warning him that if "one drop of Christian blood" is shed, Shylock's "lands and goods" will be confiscated by "the state of Venice."

Shylock realizes that he has been foiled. Thus he says that he is now willing to take Bassanio's offer of three times the amount of the bond. Portia decides otherwise. Shylock shall have "nothing but the penalty"—"just a pound of flesh"—no more, no less. And if he takes even "in the estimation of a hair" more than a pound of flesh, he will die and all his goods will be confiscated. Gratiano jeers at the moneylender; now the tables are turned. Realizing that he is beaten at his own game, Shylock asks for only the amount of the bond—and Bassanio offers it—but Portia points out that all the court was witness to Shylock's refusing the money. Therefore, he can have "nothing but the forfeiture," which he can still take, but at his own peril. In addition, Portia reminds Shylock that one of the laws of Venice forbids an alien from directly or indirectly attempting "to seek the life of any citizen" of Venice. She tells Shylock that she has seen sufficient proof that Shylock seeks Antonio's life both directly *and* indirectly. Thus, she commands him to "beg mercy of the Duke." At this point, the Duke speaks and pardons Shylock, sparing his life and adding that the penalty of the state's taking half of Shylock's goods will be reduced if Shylock evidences some "humbleness." Shylock is adamant at such a proposal: "Nay, take my life and all," he declares.

Following the Duke's merciful example, Antonio says that he will take only half of Shylock's goods which are due to him (Shylock can have the other half) in trust in order to give them to Lorenzo (Shylock's son-in-law) upon Shylock's death, on two conditions: first, Shylock must become a Christian, and second, he must deed everything to Jessica and Lorenzo. Quietly, Shylock agrees to the settlement: "I am content," he says and asks permission to leave the court.

The Duke invites Portia to dinner, but she declines; she also declines Bassanio's offer of three thousand ducats as her legal fee. Both Antonio and Bassanio press Portia to take something; they are both exceedingly grateful for all she has done, and Portia finally agrees to take two tokens as a "remembrance." She asks for Bassanio's gloves, and she also asks for his ring. Bassanio pales; she can ask for anything, he says, but ask not for his ring. It was a present from his wife, who made him promise never to part with it. Portia pretends indignation: she wants "nothing else" but the ring; "methinks I have a mind to it." She tells Bassanio that he is only "liberal in offers." He is, in effect, asking her to *beg* for the ring – an insult. Turning, she leaves. Antonio pleads with his friend; surely the lawyer deserves the ring. At last, Bassanio yields and sends Gratiano after the lawyer to give him the ring. He then turns to Antonio and tells him that early the next morning they will "fly toward Belmont."

Commentary

We now reach the dramatic high point of the play. In this scene, the matter of the "bond" reaches its crisis and its resolution: Shylock is defeated, Antonio is saved, and the lovers are free to return to Belmont; thus, Shakespeare gives us the happy ending which a romantic comedy requires.

In the introductory speeches by the Duke and Antonio, we are reminded of the antithetical positions of the two adversaries. The Duke of Venice himself calls Shylock "an inhuman wretch,/ Uncapable of pity," and Antonio characterizes himself as lost – "no lawful means" can save him. Sympathy surrounds Antonio, but dramatic sympathy is also structured around the solitary figure of Shylock. He is an intensely sympathetic figure here, alone in his solitude, surrounded on all sides by his enemies. This will be even more striking at the moment of his defeat.

By asking Shylock to show mercy toward Antonio, the Duke provides Shylock with a final opportunity to restate his position and, dramatically, Shakespeare prolongs the suspense of whether or not Shylock will actually demand Antonio's life. Throughout this scene Shylock is asked, both by the court and by his opponents *why* he refuses to relent toward Antonio. In each case, his answers are themselves unanswerable; he "stands upon the law"; the law is a creation of those who are now asking him to break it. Shylock's principles are as good, and better, than his inquisitors; it is under *their* law that he has "sworn/ To have the due and forfeit of my bond." However, Shylock goes beyond this and, in effect, he admits that his desire for revenge lies in the "lodged hate" that he bears toward Antonio. Although he professes to stand on the letter of the law, Shylock reveals quite clearly that his real motive has nothing to do with right or wrong, justice or injustice, but with his desire to destroy another human being – a Christian who has publicly scorned and spit upon him. This admission is important, since it figures later in Portia's plea, in her powerful "quality of mercy" speech.

Antonio knows that mercy is unlikely from Shylock, and Shakespeare tightens the tension of this scene by having Antonio beseech Bassanio to stop trying to win any sympathy from Shylock. It is no use; Shylock insists upon having justice carried out according to the law. Yet, while Shylock is demanding "justice," Shakespeare makes absolutely clear to the audience that Shylock's inhumanity, his obsession with revenge, is what motivates his demands. When Shylock says, "the pound of flesh. . . . is dearly bought, is mine, and I will have it," he is not speaking of "rights" anymore; he is demanding his enemy's blood.

Tension increases further when Nerissa (as the law clerk) is announced, and she presents the letter from Bellario to the Duke. Tension increases almost unbearably as the Duke reads the letter and Shylock pulls out his knife and begins to sharpen it on the sole of his shoe. It is an almost melodramatic touch, giving Shylock's inhumanity powerful, visible form. Shylock now seems in complete command, secure in the knowledge that, legally, he has bested everyone in the courtroom. He, an alien Jew, in a Christian community that has spurned him, has triumphed over prejudice and has won in a Venetian court because of the binding integrity of Venetian law.

When Portia is brought on in disguise, Shakespeare sustains the tension still longer by having her question the legality of the bond – Antonio may not have agreed formally or he may have agreed to another set of conditions. Her question "Do you confess the bond?" emphasizes once more that no avenue of escape is possible for Antonio. He answers that he agreed to the bond. The "quality of mercy" speech that follows is a last plea; seemingly, Portia sees no other hope for Antonio. Thus, she confirms the "decree established," and this gives her yet one moment more to think of some new strategy. In a moment of inspiration, she asks to see the bond; she inspects it, and she discerns a *flaw*: Antonio's *flesh* may be forfeit, but nothing has been stipulated concerning the letting of *blood*. Thus she, like Shylock, decides to stand on the absolute letter of Venetian law: Shylock may indeed claim "a pound of flesh, to be by him cut off/ Nearest the merchant's heart." She can declare this, knowing full well that Shylock's knife will never touch Antonio. This explains her surprisingly legal coldness; Portia knows *exactly* what she is doing. At this point, however, the audience doesn't, and this, of course, adds to the tension of the scene.

Thus she proceeds with methodical legality—until the last moment, when she says, understatedly, "Tarry a little; there is something else," words which will reverse the whole situation. Now it can be demonstrated anew that Shylock remains merciless in order to justify the punishment which he finally receives. Portia's delay demonstrates this and shows us Shylock's insistence on the absolute letter of the law, for it will be in accordance with the law that Shylock will punish Antonio. When Portia orders Antonio to "lay bare your bosom," Shylock is able to quote from the bond; "So says the bond. . . . 'Nearest his heart'; those are the very words." And when Portia humanely asks Shylock to "have . . . some surgeon . . . to stop his wounds," Shylock is appalled at Portia's lack of legalese: "Is it so nominated in the bond? . . . I cannot find it; 'tis not in the bond." Clearly, Portia is leading Shylock slowly into a trap which he has prepared for himself with his reply to her plea for mercy, "My deeds upon my head! I crave the law."

At this point, the dignity which Shylock possessed at the scene's beginning and the sympathy which Shakespeare evoked for him has now gone, as he exults over Antonio's approaching death. As an avenger of past wrongs by Antonio, Shylock gained some sympathy from the audience; now, whetting his knife and anticipating with relish the moment when he will be able to use it, he becomes a butcher and loses that sympathy. All of this is necessary for the total effect of the play; this is why Shakespeare wisely makes

Portia delay final pronouncements and then ingeniously begin to reveal new interpretations of absolute justice. Shakespeare is manipulating, with genius, the sympathy of the audience.

Antonio's seemingly last speech at line 263 has a dignified nobility; he declares once more his love for Bassanio; he asks him neither to grieve nor repent. At this point, the situation is a potentially tragic one, and once more Shakespeare needs to remind his audience that this play is *not*, finally, tragic. He achieves this at the moment of greatest tension when he allows the drama to slacken for a moment, and we listen in on the little exchange between the disguised wives (Portia and Nerissa) as their husbands declare their love and loyalty for one another; we chuckle when we hear Portia and Nerissa comment on these "last" words between Antonio and Bassanio. The "judge" and the "clerk" agree that the *wives* of these two gentlemen would *not* be happy to hear their husbands exchange such avowals of ready sacrifice of lives for one another.

The turning point of this act and of the play occurs at line 304: "Tarry a little; there is something else." Obviously, Shylock has come toward Antonio and now stands with his knife raised to strike, while the group on stage stands transfixed. Portia's voice, still calm, cuts through the silence. With Portia's pronouncement that the law allows "no jot of blood," Shylock's case is lost. He is almost struck dumb; "Is that the law?" is all he can ask. He was absolutely certain that his trust in the law was inviolate. The law that he believed to be so solid crumbles before him, and he realizes that his case is now absolutely, irrevocably reversed.

The law goes on to condemn him, reversing his position so completely that he himself is threatened with death. Shylock's last appearance before us, in total defeat, can, in some cases, depending on the actor, win back some of the sympathy lost earlier in this scene. But he is given little to say in comment upon the judgment passed upon him. Here, silence is the most powerful kind of eloquence. One can hardly imagine his next-to-the-last line, "I am content," uttered in any other way than in almost a whisper. He has been defeated—he, a Jew—in a Venetian, Christian court of law, and as part of his punishment, he has had to agree to become a Christian. This is an ultimate punishment for so orthodox a Jew; he is so stunned that he *begs* his judges: "I pray you give me leave to go from hence:/ I am not well. Send the deed after me,/ And I will sign it."

This is a masterstroke of simple, understated pathos. Now, Shylock has lost everything. He has shown us, however, how hate breeds hate, and Shakespeare has demonstrated how hate is finally, ultimately, defeated. Through Shylock's extreme behavior, Shakespeare dramatizes the way in which the laws of justice and property on which society is based can be, without charity and mercy and humanity, as ferocious as the law of any jungle. This, then, rather than the legal quibbles, is what is important in this scene. There is no denying that the rule of law is necessary. But law, when it is not tempered with *mercy*, is, as Shakespeare vividly shows us, both inhuman and destructive.

Since this is the central scene of the play and since it turns on our interpretation of Shylock, it follows that the way we see Shylock here determines the way we see the whole play. If he is played as a near-tragic figure, the conflict between mercy and justice is to some extent obscured. Shylock is left stripped of his daughter, his property, and his religion. That seems a harsh judgment; at times, it is difficult to see Shylock as anything but a figure of pathos. We tend to agree with the nineteenth-century writer Hazlitt, who wrote that "certainly our sympathies are oftener with him than with his enemies. He is honest in his vices; they are hypocrites in their virtues." On this point, we ought to recall three things. First, for the Elizabethan audience, Shylock was not just a "characterization"; he was the "villain" of a romantic comedy, and as such, he has to be punished. Second, Shylock's money, which he had hoarded for himself, is to go to Lorenzo and Jessica, two of the play's lovers. Love and hate are thematically opposed in this play, and since Shylock is slowly revealed to be the embodiment of hate, there is a satisfying kind of justice in his riches going to a pair of lovers. And third, the court's judgment that Shylock become a Christian would have pleased the Elizabethan audience immensely. They all genuinely believed that only a Christian could achieve salvation; they would see the court's decision as a chance for Shylock to achieve salvation. Thus the judgment was imposed, quite literally, for the good of Shylock's soul.

After Shylock's exit, the play, which has, at times, come near to tragedy, and which has had, because of Shylock, an element of pathos, reverts completely to the tone of a romantic comedy. The barrier to the true fulfillment of love has been removed. It remains only for us to return to Belmont for the closing act of the play; the threats and conflicts of this act are removed and are replaced by an atmosphere of love and concord.

ACT IV – SCENE 2

Summary

Still in Venice after the trial, Portia stops on a street and instructs Nerissa to find Shylock's house and have him sign the deed bequeathing everything he owns to Lorenzo and Jessica; then they will be home by tomorrow.

Gratiano catches up with them and presents Portia with the ring from Bassanio, who, he says, also sends an invitation to dinner. Portia accepts the ring, but declines the dinner invitation. She asks Gratiano, however, to show Nerissa ("my youth") the way to "old Shylock's house." Nerissa, in an aside, whispers to Portia that on the way she will try to get the ring which she gave to *her* husband on their wedding day, a ring which she made him "swear to keep for ever." Portia is delighted at her friend's plan. She is certain that Nerissa will succeed, and then both of them will have a merry time hearing their husbands try to explain how and why they gave their wedding rings away to other men.

Commentary

This act's final, brief scene continues the previous scene's closing mood; it is really its conclusion. By this point in the play, we are absolutely sure that Portia and Nerissa will both "outface" and "outswear" the men. It is almost a commonplace that in every one of Shakespeare's romantic comedies, the women emerge as shrewder and wittier than the men. Portia is one of those Shakespearean heroines. She is not only superior to all of the men in the climactic scene in word – but she also excels them in deed. It is she who plans and executes Antonio's deliverance and sees that merciful justice is carried out.

ACT V – SCENE 1

Summary

It is a moonlight night at Belmont, and Lorenzo and Jessica are on the avenue leading to Portia's house. In the still evening air, the newlyweds are jokingly comparing this night to nights when other lovers – Troilus, Thisbe, Dido, and Medea – all committed romantic acts of love and daring. Lorenzo reminds Jessica that this night is very much like the night when he "stole" Jessica away, and she reminds him that on just such a night as this, Lorenzo swore his vows of love to her. She boasts that she could surpass him in producing other examples of other lovers, but she hears someone approaching. It is Stephano, who brings them news that Portia, accompanied by Nerissa, will arrive "before break of day." Launcelot then comes in, dancing and "hooloaing" and "sollaing" that his master Bassanio will arrive before morning, and he exits.

Lorenzo asks Stephano to have the musicians come outdoors and play. Silently, Portia and Nerissa enter and pause to listen. Portia remarks that music heard at night "sounds much sweeter than by day." Lorenzo hears Portia's voice and recognizes it immediately. He welcomes her home, and Portia gives orders that no one is to mention her absence. Then, as dawn is about to break, a trumpet announces the arrival of Bassanio, Antonio, Gratiano, and their followers.

Portia and Bassanio immediately exchange loving greetings, and Bassanio introduces his friend Antonio, who is graciously welcomed. Their conversation, however, is interrupted by a quarrel between Nerissa and Gratiano over the wedding ring which she gave him, and which he now confesses to have given to a "judge's clerk," a half-grown youth no taller than Nerissa. Portia tells Gratiano that he was at fault to give away his "wife's first gift." She is confident that Bassanio would *never*, for any reason, part with the ring which she gave him. Angrily, Gratiano tells her that Bassanio did *indeed* give away his wedding ring; in fact, he gave it to the "judge that begg'd it," just as he, Bassanio, gave his ring to the judge's clerk. Both wives pretend shock and anger, and they vow never to sleep with their husbands until they see their wedding rings again. Bassanio pleads in vain that he gave his ring for good reason to the lawyer who saved Antonio's life. Well, says Portia, since you have been so generous to *him*, if that lawyer comes here, "I'll have [him] for my bedfellow." "And," adds Nerissa, "I his clerk."

Antonio is terribly disturbed as he witnesses Portia's fury; he feels that he is "the unhappy subject of these quarrels." Bassanio then swears that if Portia will forgive him this time, he will never break a promise to her again. Antonio speaks up and offers his soul as forfeit, as before he offered his body, in support of Bassanio. Portia accepts Antonio's soul as security for Bassanio's word. "Give him this [ring]," she tells Antonio, "and bid him keep it better than the other." In amazement, Bassanio recognizes it as the same ring which he gave the lawyer. Nerissa then returns Gratiano's ring to her husband, who receives it in similar amazement.

Portia then explains that it was she who was the lawyer Balthasar at the trial of Antonio, and Nerissa was her clerk; they have just returned from Venice. For Antonio, she has a letter containing good news – three of Antonio's ships have safely come into port. Antonio reads the letter himself and is ecstatic: "Sweet lady, you have given me life and living," he says. Nerissa then presents Shylock's deed to Lorenzo and Jessica, bequeathing them all of his possessions.

"It is almost morning," Portia observes, and it will take time to explain how all these things happened. "Let us go in," she says, and she and Nerissa will answer all questions.

Commentary

Act IV was given over almost entirely to the threat posed to the romantic love theme and was dominated by the figure of Shylock. In the play's last act, consisting of only this scene, we return to Belmont – the world of comedy and romance. The opening dialogue between Lorenzo and Jessica reestablishes the atmosphere of harmony.

Lorenzo's opening words call upon us to imagine that the lovers are surrounded by night and moonlight, "when the sweet wind did gently kiss the trees." Their dialogue is used to create the general atmosphere of love and night and moonlight, thus establishing the tone of the scene. Lorenzo introduces the theme of love and moonlight with two speeches of great beauty. In the early lines of the act (lines 55-65), he introduces the idea that music is the "music of the spheres." This was a popular Elizabethan notion, according to which the revolution of each planet around the earth produced a sound, and the combination of all the individual sounds of the planets made a "divine harmony."

Lorenzo's next speech also concerns music. Having summoned Portia's own personal musicians, he signals them to play, and he elaborates on the nature of music to Jessica. Significantly, music is very often an important element in Shakespeare's plays, both as a theatrical device and also as a general criterion of character. Those characters who dislike music are invariably incomplete or distorted human beings. Here, Lorenzo underlines the idea that "the man that hath no music in himself. . . . Let no such man be trusted."

The arrival of Portia and Nerissa, and then of Bassanio, Gratiano, and Antonio, sets in motion the final movement of the play: the denouement of the "ring story." Shakespeare has been quietly preparing us for this story as far back as Act III, Scene 2, when Portia presented her ring to Bassanio, "Which when you part from, lose, or give away,/ Let be my vantage to exclaim upon you." The audience, of course, has been anticipating this development since the first scene of Act IV, when Antonio prevailed upon Bassanio to give the ring to "the young doctor of Rome."

After Bassanio, Antonio, and Portia converse sweetly together, Nerissa begins to take Gratiano to task, and their words suggest the beginning of a fairly violent disagreement. When Gratiano says, "By yonder moon, I swear you do me wrong," he invokes an air of injured innocence. One of the comic elements in what follows lies in the righteous confusion into which Bassanio and Gratiano are thrown. While they admit to having, for what seemed – at that particular time – to be the *best* of reasons, they did indeed part with their wedding rings. But they cannot understand their wives' furious accusations that they gave them to other women. Of course, in the comedies of ancient Greece and even in today's comedies, the sight of a man wrongly accused by his wife, yet totally unable to defend himself, is sure-fire comedy, and it is given a thorough workout here. As Nerissa berates Gratiano, Portia delivers her speech, with pious confidence, to the effect that her husband would *never*, on any account, part with the wedding ring which she gave him. Almost unconsciously, we wince in sympathy with Bassanio when he turns aside and says: "Why I were best to cut my left hand off/ And swear I lost the ring defending it."

The element of the comedy here lies in the irony of many of the lines – that is, the knowledge which the two women have and the knowledge which the audience has and the knowledge which the two husbands do *not* have. This produces some lines which sound horrifyingly improper to the two husbands, but are quite literally true. Portia says, for example, of the "doctor" to whom Bassanio gave the ring, that if he comes "near my house. . . . I'll not deny him anything I have,/ No, not my body nor my husband's bed. . . . I'll have that doctor for my bedfellow." To which Nerissa adds, sassily, "And I his clerk." And further, when they return the rings, Portia is able to affirm "For by this ring the doctor lay with me," to which infidelity Nerissa is again able to add, the "doctor's clerk." By this time Bassanio and Gratiano have been teased enough, and the end of the scene is a succession of revelations: first, the true identity of the lawyer and his clerk, then of Antonio's good fortune, and finally, of Lorenzo and Jessica's inheritance.

Ending the comedy with the ring story serves two purposes. In the first place, Bassanio and Gratiano discover who Antonio's true saviors were. Second, and more important, there is always the threat of anticlimax at the end of a romantic comedy, when all the loose ends are tied up and the lovers are all reunited; suddenly, the "sweet talk" can become unbearably insipid. This is uniquely, usually, not the case with Shakespeare. He had a keen sense of the bawdy, and here he tempers his romantic scene with salty comedy in order to suggest that these lovers are very human lovers; their marriages will have their misunderstandings, but all this can be overcome with the aid of love and with another ingredient, a good sense of humor.

CHARACTER ANALYSES

Antonio

Although the plot turns on Antonio's predicament, his character is not sharply drawn. He is a rich man, and a comfortable man, and a popular man, but still he suffers from an inner sadness. One obvious, dramatic reason for Antonio's quiet melancholy is simply that Shakespeare cannot give Antonio too much to do or say without taking away valuable dialogue time from his major characters. Therefore, Shakespeare makes Antonio a quiet, dignified figure.

One of Antonio's most distinguishing characteristics is his generosity. He is more than happy to offer his good credit standing so that Bassanio can go to Belmont in the latest fashions in order to court Portia. And one of the reasons why Shylock hates Antonio so intensely is that Antonio has received Shylock's borrowers by lending them money at the last minute to pay off Shylock; and Antonio never charges interest. He is only too happy to help his friends, but he would never stoop to accepting more than the original amount in return. Antonio's generosity is boundless, and for Bassanio, he is willing to go to the full length of friendship, even if it means that he himself may suffer for it.

Antonio is an honorable man. When he realizes that Shylock is within his lawful rights, Antonio is ready to fulfill the bargain he entered into to help Bassanio. "The Duke cannot deny the course of the law," he says. And later, he adds that he is "arm'd/ To suffer, with a quietness of spirit. . . . For if the Jew do cut but deep enough,/ I'll pay it presently with all my heart."

Antonio's courage and goodness are finally rewarded; at the end of the play, when the three pairs of lovers are reunited and happiness abounds at Belmont, Portia delivers a letter to Antonio in which he learns that the remainder of his ships has returned home safely to port.

Bassanio

Bassanio's character is more fully drawn than Antonio's, but it does not possess the powerful individuality that Shakespeare gives to his portraits of Portia and Shylock. First off, when one begins considering Bassanio, one should dismiss all the critics who condemn him for his financial habits. Bassanio's request to Antonio for more money is perfectly natural for him. He is young; he is in love; and he is, by nature, impulsive and romantic. Young men in love have often gone into debt; thus Bassanio has always borrowed money and, furthermore, no moral stigma should be involved. Shakespeare needs just such a character in this play for his plot.

If Bassanio is not a powerful hero, he is certainly a sympathetic one. First, he has some of the most memorable verse in the play — language which has music, richness, and dignity. Second, he shows us his immediate, uncalculated generosity and love; this is especially obvious when Bassanio, who has just won Portia, receives the letter telling him of Antonio's danger. Bassanio is immediately and extremely concerned over the fate of Antonio and is anxious to do whatever is possible for his friend. Here, the situation is melodramatic and calls for a romantic, seemingly impossible, rescue mission.

When at last Bassanio and Portia are reunited, he speaks forthrightly and truthfully to her. He refuses to implicate Antonio, even though it was at Antonio's urging that he gave away his wedding ring to the judge who cleverly saved Antonio's life: "If you did know," he tells Portia, "for what I gave the ring/ And how unwillingly I left the ring, . . . You would abate the strength of your displeasure." No matter how powerful the circumstances, he admits that he was wrong to part with the ring because he had given his oath to Portia to keep it. As the play ends, Bassanio's impetuous nature is once more stage-center. Speaking to his wife, he vows: "Portia, forgive me this enforced wrong; . . . and by my soul I swear/ I never more will break an oath with thee." Of course, he will; this, however, is part of Bassanio's charm. He means it with all his heart when he swears to Portia, but when the next opportunity arises and he is called on to rashly undertake some adventure full of dash and daring, he'll be off. Portia knows this also and loves him deeply, despite this minor flaw.

Portia

Portia is the romantic heroine of the play, and she must be presented on the stage with much beauty and intelligence. Of her beauty, we need no convincing. Bassanio's words are enough; thus we turn to her love for Bassanio. Already she has given him cause to think that it is possible that he can woo and win her, for on an earlier visit to Belmont, Bassanio did "receive fair speechless messages" from her eyes. And when Nerissa mentions the fact that Bassanio might possibly be a suitor, Portia tries to disguise her anxiety, but she fails. Nerissa understands her mistress. Portia is usually very self-controlled, but she reveals her anxiety concerning Bassanio a little later when he has arrived at her mansion and is about to choose one of the caskets. She has fallen in love with him, and her anxiety and confusion undo her. "Pause a day or two," she begs, for "in choosing wrong,/ I lose your company. . . ." She thus makes sure that he knows that it is not hate that she feels for him.

Bassanio's correct choice of the casket overwhelms Portia. She wishes she had more of everything to give Bassanio: "This house, these servants and this same myself/ Are yours, my lord: I give them with this ring. . . ." She willingly shares all she owns with Bassanio. Once master of her emotions, she has fallen completely under the spell of love's madness. Love is a reciprocal giving and receiving, and so it is with perfect empathy that she sends her beloved away almost immediately to try and save his friend Antonio. They will be married, but their love will not be consummated until his friend is saved, if possible.

Portia's second characteristic that is most readily apparent is her graciousness — that is, her tact and sympathy. Despite her real feelings about the Prince of Morocco, Portia answers him politely and reassuringly. Since the irony of her words is not apparent to him, his feelings are spared. She tells him that he is "as fair/ As any comer I have look'd on yet/ For my affection." She shows Morocco the honor his rank deserves. But once he is gone, she reveals that she did *not* like him. "A gentle riddance," she says, "Draw the curtains."

When the Prince of Arragon arrives, Portia carefully addresses him with all the deference due his position. She calls him "noble." But after he has failed and has left, she cries out, "O, these deliberate fools!" To her, both of these men are shallow and greedy and self-centered; yet to their faces, she is as ladylike as possible. Lorenzo appreciates this gentle generosity of spirit; when Portia has allowed her new husband to leave to try and help his best friend out of his difficulty, he says to her: "You have a noble and a true conceit/ Of god-like amity."

In the courtroom, Portia (in disguise) speaks to Shylock about mercy, but this is not merely an attempt to stall; she truly means what she says. It is an eloquent appeal she makes. Her request for mercy comes from her habitual goodness. She hopes, of course, to soften his heart, knowing the outcome if he refuses. But the words come from her heart, honestly and openly and naturally.

Finally, of course, what we most remember about Portia, after the play is over, is her wit and her playfulness. Even when Portia is complaining to Nerissa about the terms of her father's will, she does so wittily: "Is it not hard, Nerissa, that I cannot choose one nor refuse none?" And then she ticks off, like a computer, the eccentricities of the six suitors who have arrived at Belmont to try for her hand. They are either childish, humorless, volatile, ignorant, too fantastically dressed, weak, or have a drinking problem. She is clearly glad to be rid of them all when it is announced that they are departing.

We recall too the humorous way that she imagines dressing like a man and aping the mannerisms of all of the men she has observed in her short life. She bets Nerissa that she can out-man any man when it comes to swaggering and playing the macho bit: "I have within my mind/ A thousand raw tricks of these bragging Jacks,/ Which I will practise." Men are as transparent as stale beer to her; she revels in turning the tables and having a bit of fun even while she is on a daring mission to try and save Antonio's life. And even in the courtroom, when Bassanio extravagantly offers his life for Antonio's, Portia quips in an aside that "Your wife would give you little thanks for that,/ If she were by, to hear you make the offer."

The entire ring plot is Portia's idea, and she and Nerissa relish the prospect of the jest at their husbands' expense. Bassanio swears over and over that he never gave his ring away to another woman (and he is more than a little embarrassed to admit that he gave it to another man), but with a fine sense of comedy, Portia plays the role of the "angry wife" just as well as she played the role of the "learned young lawyer" at Antonio's trial.

Only when Portia first falls in love with Bassanio does she lose all self-control; once she regains control of herself, she takes matters in hand until the very end of the play, and there she displays total command of the situation. "You are all amazed," she tells them, and then she shows them a letter from Padua, explaining everything, and she gaily invites them inside where she will continue to explain and entertain. She is a delightful creature, one of Shakespeare's most intelligent and captivating heroines.

Shylock

Shylock is the most vivid and memorable character in *The Merchant of Venice*, and he is one of Shakespeare's greatest dramatic creations. On stage, it is Shylock who makes the play, and almost all of the great actors of the English and Continental stage have attempted the role. But the character of Shylock has also been the subject of much critical debate: how are we meant to evaluate the attitude of the Venetians in the play toward him? Or his attitude toward them? Is he a bloodthirsty villain? Or is he a man "more sinned against than sinning"? One of the reasons that such questions arise is that there are really two stage Shylocks in the play: first, there is the stage "villain" who is required for the *plot*; second, there is the human being who suffers the loss of his daughter, his property, and, very importantly for him, his religion.

Shylock's function in this play is to be the obstacle, the man who stands in the way of the love stories; such a man is a traditional figure in romantic comedies. Something or someone must impede young, romantic love; here, it is Shylock and the many and various ways that he is linked to the three sets of lovers. The fact that he is a Jew is, in a sense, accidental. Shakespeare wanted to contrast liberality against selfishness – in terms of money and in terms of love. There was such a figure available from the literature of the time, one man who could fulfill both functions: this man would be a usurer, or moneylender, with a beautiful daughter that he held onto as tightly as he did his ducats. Usury was *forbidden* to Christians by the church of the Middle Ages, and as a consequence, moneylending was controlled by the Jews; as a rule, it was usually the *only* occupation which the law allowed to them. As a result, a great deal of medieval literature produced the conventional figure of the Jewish moneylender, usually as a minor character, but also too, as a major character. It is from this medieval literary tradition that Shakespeare borrows the figure of Shylock, just as Marlowe did for his *Jew of Malta*. Some commentators have said that the character of Shylock is an example of Elizabethan (and Shakespeare's own) anti-Semitism. In contrast, many have seen the creation of Shylock as an *attack* on this kind of intolerance. But Shakespeare, they forget, was a dramatist. He was not concerned with either anti- nor pro-Semitism, except in the way it shaped individual characters in his plays to produce the necessary drama that he was attempting to create. The play is thus emphatically *not* anti-Semitic; rather, because of the nature of Shylock's involvement in the love plots, it is *about* anti-Semitism. Shakespeare never seriously defined or condemned a group through the presentation of an individual; he only

did this for the purposes of comedy by creating caricatures in miniature for our amusement. Shylock is drawn in bold strokes; he is
meant to be a "villain" in terms of the romantic comedy, but because
of the multi-dimensionality which Shakespeare gives him, we are
meant to sympathize with him at times, loathe him at others.
Shakespeare's manipulation of our emotions regarding Shylock is a
testament to his genius as a creator of character.

When Shylock leaves the courtroom in Act IV, Scene 1, he is
stripped of all that he has. He is a defeated man. Yet we cannot
feel deep sympathy for him — some, perhaps, but not much.
Shakespeare's intention was not to make Shylock a tragic figure; instead, Shylock was meant to function as a man who could be vividly
realized as the epitomy of selfishness; he must be defeated in this
romantic comedy. In a sense, it is Shakespeare's own brilliance
which led him to create Shylock as almost too human. Shylock is
powerfully drawn, perhaps too powerfully for this comedy, but his
superb dignity is admirable, despite the fact that we must finally
condemn him. Perhaps the poet W. H. Auden has given us our best
clue as to how we must deal with Shylock: "Those to whom evil is
done," he says, "do evil in return." This explains in a few words much
of the moneylender's complexity and our complex reactions toward
him.

QUESTIONS FOR REVIEW

1. Why has the character of Shylock been interpreted in so many
   differing ways by so many different critics? Why is this dramatic character more puzzling, or more stimulating than any
   other character in any of Shakespeare's other romantic comedies?

2. Many critics feel that the images of the sea in Act I, Scene 1
   strike the keynote of the play, that they suggest the bond
   story as the central theme. Do you agree or disagree? Why?

3. What do the choice of caskets made by the Prince of Morocco
   and the Prince of Arragon show about their fitness to marry
   Portia? Explain.

4. Relate Antonio's naturally melancholy disposition, which is emphasized in the opening scene, to his stoic acceptance of misfortune when he has to forfeit the bond.

5. The famous eighteenth-century writer Samuel Johnson refers in one of his essays to the "improbability" of *The Merchant of Venice*. What qualities of the play are the most improbable?

6. The nineteenth-century poet Samuel Taylor Coleridge speaks of Shakespeare's "representation of men in all ages and all times" in this particular play. What are the universal or timeless elements in it?

7. Compare the argument about usury (I.iii), the talk about friendship (III.ii), and the plea for mercy (IV.i) from the standpoint of dramatic intensity. Which one of these subjects, in your view, is the most important issue in this play?

8. Many critics think that *The Merchant of Venice* is more tragic than comic. Why do you think so? Or do you disagree? Why?

9. Justify Shylock's demand for revenge against Antonio.

10. From references in the play, quotes, allusions, etc., describe Venice as a setting and as a city for this play.

SELECTED BIBLIOGRAPHY

ADAMS, J. Q. *A Life of William Shakespeare.* Boston: Houghton Mifflin Co., 1923.

ALEXANDER, PETER. *Shakespeare.* Oxford: Oxford University Press, 1964.

BEVINGTON, DAVID. *Shakespeare.* Arlington Heights, Ill.: A.H.M. Publications, 1978.

BLOOM, EDWARD A., ed. *Shakespeare 1564-1964.* Providence: Brown University Press, 1964.

FARNHAM, WILLARD. *The Medieval Heritage of Elizabethan Tragedy.* Berkeley, California: University of California Press, 1936.

GIBSON, H. N. *The Shakespeare Claimants.* New York: Barnes & Noble, Inc., 1962.

HEILMAN, ROBERT B. *Magic in the Web.* Lexington, Kentucky: University of Kentucky Press, 1956.

HIBBARD, G. R. "Love, Marriage and Money in Shakespeare's Theatre and Shakespeare's England," *The Elizabethan Theatre*, Vol. 7, p. 134-55, 1979.

KANTAK, V. Y. "An Approach to Shakespearean Comedy," *Shakespeare Survey*, Vol. 22, pp. 7-14, 1974.

KNIGHT, G. WILSON. *The Wheel of Fire.* London: Oxford University Press, 1930.

LEAVIS, F. R. *The Common Pursuit.* Hardmonsworth, Middlesex: Penguin Books, Ltd., 1963.

LERNER L. *The Uses of Nostalgia.* Schocken, 1972.

SEWELL, ARTHUR. *Character and Society in Shakespeare.* Oxford: Clarendon Press, 1951.

SMITH, JAMES. *Shakespearean and Other Essays,* Cambridge, 1974.

WEISS, T. "Breath of Clowns and Kings," *Nation*, Aug. 16, 1971.

NOTES